NUCKED! 2

More Misadventures with the IDORA PARK EXPERIENCE NINJAS

NUCKED!

Couldn't put it down! Amusing and interesting "true" (embellished) stories of how one couple took on the challenge to recover artifacts from an amusement park that burned down. Highly recommended read! – *Ron*

A super fun and light-hearted book. Well worth the read! – *33YO*

Jim has humorously described their adventures as they tried to recover as much of the memorabilia as they could. One does not need to be an Idora Park Groupie to appreciate the lessons learned from each of these experiences. The chapter about "The Himmelhaffer" was by far the funniest one in the book. I would highly recommend this book. – *Linda V.*

I read the entire book in one sitting. It has everything, laughter, tears, and most importantly it brought up fond memories… Can't wait for the next book. – *Patty S.*

This book was great! I read it in an afternoon! It was well written and very funny! – *Sherry829*

Highly entertaining… – *AllTheGoodNamesWereTaken*

The authors are passionate, charming, and gifted writers. – *Anonymous*

…Once you start, you're addicted to the end. – *Anonymous*

I've been a follower on Facebook and the stories are hilarious. I had to buy the book and hear more about the adventures… Terrific writing! Action packed. – *Anonymous*

NUCKED! 2

More Misadventures with the IDORA PARK EXPERIENCE NINJAS

A Memoir... Sort of.

Written and Illustrated by:
James Amey & Toni Amey

The Idora Park Experience
Canfield, Ohio

Cover design: James & Toni Amey

To purchase this book in bulk for promotional, educational, or business use, or for other general questions, please contact The Idora Park Experience, LLC at:

E-Mail: Info@TheIdoraParkExperience.com
www.TheIdoraParkExperience.com
www.Facebook.com/TheIdoraParkExperience

Dedicated to Joe Sander

For Joe Sander and the students and staff of the Mahoning County Career &
Technical Center (MCCTC) who have contributed their time, energy, talents and
passion toward restoring and preserving the artifacts and memories of Idora Park.
Joe, your leadership, guidance and mentorship of your students has helped to mold
the future while preserving the past. You have been a joy and inspiration to work
with and your support, dedication and friendship have made the impossible
possible. Your legacy is forever imbedded with that of The Idora Park
Experience.

In Memory of Rick A. Shale

Long before we became friends with Rick Shale, his book, "Idora Park The Last Ride of Summer", was a catalyst for igniting Jim's passion to save the memories of Idora Park and it still serves as the ultimate research vessel for everything Idora Park.

We were blessed when a common interest (that may be a bit of an understatement) brought us together and then grew into a close personal friendship. And when we lost him to cancer in 2022 it was a devastating loss, not just to us and those that loved him, but to the entire Youngstown community.

Until we ride again Rick…

Table of Contents

A Note from Jim & Spike

If you read the first "Nucked! Misadventures with The Idora Park Experience Ninjas", then you know you are in for a wild ride as you join us and our ninja, Nuck, on more hilarious misadventures hunting down Idora Park artifacts. You'll meet some new outrageous characters (who may even resemble people you've experienced in your life) and encounter some far-fetched situations that may even be true. After all, this is a memoir… Sort of.

If you didn't read the first "Nucked!" book, then you will have a lot of questions that we can't even begin to answer in these few paragraphs. But here are the basics:

1. Idora Park was an amusement park in Youngstown, Ohio (1899–1984). It died as a result of injuries sustained in a devastating fire in April 1984, and from complications of a crashed Rust-Belt economy.

2. For about 30 years we have been collecting artifacts from Idora Park. What started with small inconsequential items morphed into a mission to save whatever we could find from Idora Park, regardless of where we had to go or what we had to go through to get it… well almost.

3. In 2012 Jim began posting stories on social media about our misadventures collecting the artifacts. As of the writing of this book we have more than 20,000 people who follow our misadventures online.

4. Somewhere along the way we acquired a 3'-3" broken-English speaking knucklehead ninja we named Nuck (short for knucklehead), and promptly began getting regularly "nucked" by the knucklehead… Hence the title of both books (…so far).

5. In April 2014, 30 years after the fire that took down Idora Park, we had the first public opening of our museum of Idora Park artifacts. We had more than 1,000 people attend that first opening and have had as many as 2,500 in a single weekend opening since then. (Our local government limits us to opening only a few days a year.)

6. In 2019 we wrote the book "Lost Idora Park" published by Arcadia Publishing and it is considered a success and top seller in its market. But the number one question we got was when we were going to write the book with the stories of our adventures (like Jim does on social media).

7. In 2021 we wrote "Nucked! Misadventures with The Idora Park Experience Ninjas". It received outstanding reviews and readers once again asked for more…

8. So here we are… More…

INTRODUCTION: Where we last left our heroes...

The Last Man Standing was strapped securely to my trailer. Nuck and I hopped in my truck and headed south toward home, leaving Idora's wide open Upper Midway, approaching the Lower Midway and eventually we'd leave via the back gate: Billingsgate.

Idora Park's Lower Midway is much narrower than the Upper Midway. Think of an hourglass with two glass bulbs (well, misshapen glass bulbs) and a long narrow neck between them. One "glass bulb" is the Upper Midway, located at the north end of Idora Park. The long narrow "glass neck" is the Lower Midway and farther south is another large asphalt area where some of the large rides and the Ballroom were located – the second "glass bulb" (also misshapen) of the hourglass.

NUCKED!

All of the rides, concessions, games… everything, they're all long gone now. All that remains of Idora Park is the asphalt midways, a few concrete foundation structures, a dilapidated Miniature Golf Course and the ever-encroaching weeds, trees and bushes that have even made their way through the cracked and broken asphalt. Since 1984 Mother Nature has been reclaiming what has really, always been hers.

We were just entering the Lower Midway when I caught movement from the corner of my eye. Something was in the grass and weeds to my left and moving parallel to us. There were at least a few of them and they were small. My first thought was that they were grasshopper stragglers and maybe I should swerve left and run them over with my truck. My next thought was that whatever was moving was pretty quick and bigger than a grasshopper. I didn't want to hurt any animals, so I slowed the truck. Nuck saw something too…

NUCK: (pointing and excited) Look Boss, baby clown!

ME: (confused) What? Hunh? Where? Baby clown? What are you talking about? That's probably a squirrel or opossum, maybe a rabbit. Baby clown? You crack me up!

NUCK: I see good Boss, baby clown! More than one!

Whatever Nuck saw was still moving in the weeds and it was more than just one. Finally, I saw something colorful and furry well, fuzzy looking. It poked its head up out of the weeds and looked me right in the eyes, then dropped back quickly into the underbrush. It looked like a toy and Nuck was right, it was colorful.

That was no squirrel or anything else I'd seen on four legs. Did it even have four legs? I didn't know, it moved too fast, and I didn't get to see all of its body, just that fuzzy head and colorful face. I stopped the truck and got out. Nuck got out too, went around the truck and stood next to me…

NUCK: Boss, we go in there and catch him?

ME: Are you crazy? No way I'm going in there. We don't even know what that thing was. It probably bites. You shouldn't go in there either. Did you see how fast it is?

NUCK: Boss, you not curious, find out what that is?

ME: Of course, I'm curious, but not to the point of getting bitten. Besides, it looked like there was more than one. They could have rabies or distemper or mange or something. I'll tell you what, let's circle around it, not go directly after it. Maybe it, or they, won't expect us to outflank them. I would like to get a better look. It's too bad we don't have a big fishing net or maybe we could catch one.

NUCK: Net with long, long handle so it don't bite!

ME: (correcting him) Really? So, it "don't" bite? It's "doesn't," not "don't." You used the wrong contraction. You should have said, "…so it doesn't bite!"

My English lesson was abruptly interrupted by a rustling in the weeds just off to our right. We both heard it and looked that way. A colorful toy-looking thing ran into a small clearing giving us just enough time to see its entire body. It was no taller than maybe twelve inches and had fuzz up one side of its body, over its head and down the other side. Nuck took off running after it…

NUCK: (excited) Boss, I tell you! See, baby clown.

He was right! It looked like a clown. A little clown and it was moving pretty quickly, backwards. I didn't see its legs despite it being right out in the open. Did it even have legs? It had to have legs unless it was some kind of snake, but there was no long body or tail behind or in front of that upright body. The thing moved fast with a waddling side to side forward motion. It stopped for just a split second and turned back to look at us. The front of the thing looked just like the back! It had a face on both sides. How can that be? The thing was two-faced? Nuck who was still chasing the thing saw it too…

NUCK: See Boss, two clown!

ME: No, that's just one creature not two.

My immediate thought was that a squirrel had gotten stuck in some kid's toy and couldn't get out. But I saw no legs at all. How could it move like that with no legs? Nuck wasn't having much luck trying to catch the little critter, but it was funny watching him try.

I heard a woman's voice yell out. She was standing way off the Midway, closer to a hill to my left where Idora's picnic grounds had once stood. She was looking toward Nuck and yelling at him. She looked frail and elderly, like REAL elderly, maybe in her 100s. She didn't see me since I was a good thirty yards or so away from her and her attention was focused on Nuck, who had abruptly stopped chasing that squirrel rabbit clown thing when he heard her yelling.

I quietly slipped behind the nearest tree to watch what happened next. The old lady raised one frail looking arm and pointed a bony finger my way. She said, "Don't move! I know you're there, mister!" Uh, okay. So, I guess she did see me…

OLD LADY (OL): (angry, scolding Nuck) You get away from him. He didn't hurt you. Stop chasing him!

So, the little clown animal has an owner.

ME: (apologetically) Hey, we're sorry. We weren't sure what that was and figured maybe we could catch it and free it from that toy that's stuck on its head. Is that your dog?

OL: (scoldingly) Dog? Elmer's no dog!

ME: Elmer? He's got a name. So, he's your pet what? Rabbit?

OL: Elmer's no pet either. He's his own creature. All of 'em are. Every one of 'em.

ME: (puzzled) Every one of them? Every one of what?

OL: (grinning) Every one of the ChipPunks. They don't belong to nobody.

NUCK: (returning to my side) See Boss, lady say "don't," not "doesn't!"

ME: (shaking my head in disbelief) No kidding. She said it in the correct context. You didn't. Now please, shut up!

I looked at the old lady again and saw that the thing she called Elmer had crept up behind her and was looking at Nuck and me. It didn't look like it could possibly be alive. It looked like a puppet, but it really was alive, and it looked so familiar to me. I just couldn't place where or when I'd seen one of these…

ME: (addressing the old lady) What did you call it, a ChipPunk? Just what is a ChipPunk and how many of them are there?

OL: (lowering her voice and walking toward me with a sinister looking smile on her face and whispering slowly) You're about to find out mister. They have you surrounded…

The way the old lady said those words made the hair on the back of my neck stand up. I was leery of what I might see if I turned around. Maybe I should just run? But I'd be leaving Nuck behind and all alone to fend for himself. So many thoughts… What to do?

I didn't hear them sneak up behind me, but I could hear the thrum-like noise that they were making back there. Was it a unified chant, a song maybe? The chant got progressively louder, but no way was I going to turn around to see how many of them were there. Maybe if I just stood still and pretended that I wasn't scared they'd go away? You know, like when a big dog comes charging at you and you stand your ground the dog thinks to itself, "Oh, okay he's cool. He didn't run, no bite for me today. Maybe the next guy…"

The chanting got louder, and I could make out the words. It was a song all right, a song that I know,

"Little Bunny Foo-Foo…"

Oh yeah, I know this song.

The song continued, "… hopping through the forest, picking up the field mice…"

Yes, I used to sing this cute little song to my kids when they were young.

"… and biting off their heads."

Wait, what?

That's not how I remember that song! Biting off their heads? Bunny Foo-Foo doesn't bite off field mice heads! My thoughts were interrupted by a tugging at my pant leg. I had to see what was pulling on my pants. I looked straight down at the ground, at my feet. A small furry headed ChipPunk thing had ahold of both pant legs and was looking up from between my legs with this evil smile on its face.

I heard the old lady speak…

OL: They ain't angry yet. You'll know they's angry if they start singing, "My Little Pony!"

What's evil about the "My Little Pony" song? And why are these ChipPunks surrounding us? What exactly are these things and where did they come from? Who is this old lady and what's her relationship with them? I had so many questions…

CHIPPUNKS... The Rest of the Story

If you didn't read the Introduction now would be a really good time to do so. The rest of this just won't make any sense if you don't know where we last left our heroes... In fact, if you didn't read the first "NUCKED!", you're gonna want to... I mean how else are you gonna know what the Last Man Standing is and why we were fighting a battle with The Big Uglies on the Idora Park property? Or, for that matter, who the heck Nuck is!?

Go ahead, we'll wait right here for you.

All done? Great! Now let's get to the rest of the ChipPunk story.

Nuck was watching me while the ChipPunk named Elmer was just a few feet from where Nuck was standing. Elmer didn't appear to be threatening at all, not like the thing that was holding onto my pant legs and sneering up at me. Why did it have to be me who always gets the angry one? I worried that this ChipPunk might start climbing up my legs and how it would respond to my reaction should that actually happen. Would it try to bite me? How was I to know?

I fought the urge to panic and swat the thing away. I'd cross my legs, but that might make it mad. So, I did nothing. I looked down at the creature as it started climbing up my legs. I felt the sweat run down my back. I looked down as it climbed closer to my crotch, its' open mouth baring razor sharp teeth and the name imprinted on its' body; 8 BALL.

Seriously? The one ChipPunk that decides to climb toward my private parts has razor sharp teeth and is named 8 BALL? I was close to panic. I wondered if 8 BALL earned its' name the way fighter pilots earn "Kill" insignia on their cockpit after shooting down an enemy plane.

The old lady spoke and interrupted my thoughts.

OL: I know you must be wondering where these little fellas come from and why they's here at Idora Park. Would ya like me to fill ya in?

NUCK: (interrupting and pointing at Elmer) Boss, I keep this one? He friendly!

ME: No, you heard the lady. They aren't pets. Sorry ma'am, yes, we'd like to know more about these ChipPunks, but can you get this one to let go of me? It's freaking me out. I don't know if it's going to bite me or what he's planning on doing. Can you please just call this thing off me?

The old lady smiled and nodded at 8 BALL who let go of my pants and backed away. She obviously held some sway over the creatures. I was still too scared to turn around to see where he went or how many of them were behind me. Ignorance can be blissful. I saw occasional movement in the weeds in front of me and to my left and right, so I knew there were quite a few of the things, but I'd really only seen the two ChipPunks, Elmer and 8 BALL the pants climber. Nuck must have been reading my mind…

NUCK: So many ChipPunk here, maybe 100 behind you. Boss, maybe Elmer come home with us?

ME: (gulp) 100 behind me?

That did it, I turned around and there they were, maybe not quite a hundred, but definitely dozens of them. All were fuzzy along the top of their head and down their sides with colorful faces and bodies. One of them turned around and it had the same look and coloring as it did on its' backside.

They were all two-faced! The difference between the two sides being one side was a pale yellow and the other a bit faded and whitened, like it had been bleached by the sun. But facial and body markings were the same on both sides of each individual ChipPunk. Which side was the front, and which was the back? I couldn't tell. I realized then that these ChipPunks looked a lot like Knock Down Punks you'd throw a baseball at in a carnival or amusement park. Idora had one of those booths. It was called Hit The Kittens. I didn't see any Kittens in this group though, just punks. Well, not punks, but ChipPunks. I ignored Nuck's questions. He wasn't getting a pet ChipPunk. The old lady spoke again…

OL: Many of Idora Park's buildings stood for a few years after the old park closed. Left abandoned the buildings deteriorated, the midways cracked, weeds grew everywhere. Mother Nature wanted the land. With no humans around the wildlife returned. Deer now run the hills. They's raccoons, opossum, squirrels and even a few monkeys – descendants of the great monkey escape of 1947.

I knew about the Great Monkey Escape of 1947. Idora created Monkey Island in 1928. It was a shed in the middle of a concrete pond. The shed was home for dozens of monkeys. In the summer of '47 the monkeys decided it was time for a jailbreak. Maybe they just wanted time off? Some monkeys were recaptured fairly quickly, some climbed up on the Fun House roof and threw feces at park goers.

NUCKED!

Yes, feces! Poop! I guess that's what monkeys do for fun after being cooped up.

Some of the monkeys left for the adjoining park land, Mill Creek Park. Occasionally there would be reports that a monkey or two would be spotted in Mill Creek Park. When winter arrived in 1947 the monkeys that hadn't already been captured returned to their cage in Idora Park to escape the cold. Well, except for four of them, those monkeys were never accounted for. Was the old lady telling us that monkeys from the '47 Great Monkey Escape or more likely, their descendants were somewhere in Idora Park? The thought caused me to look up and scan the tree branches, but no monkeys were in sight.

Back to the story…

ME: Yes, I knew about the monkeys, but what's the story on the ChipPunks? And why is it that I've never heard of them before now? I've been in Idora Park numerous times, and I've never got a glimpse of one until now, yet there seems to be dozens and dozens of them. How come no one has reported seeing them? Lots of people stroll through these grounds. Where did they come from, what are they and how many of them are there?

OL: The ChipPunks keep to themselves. The only reason why you know about them now is because you made so much noise shooting off those firecrackers at a bunch of grasshoppers. There are two things that ChipPunks hate, loud noise and baseballs.

ME: Baseballs! Aha! I knew it! These are Knock Down Punks, aren't they? But how do they move? Battery powered? They are so realistic, as if they are alive.

OL: (angry again) You really do not listen, do you? They ARE alive! They's from here, Idora Park. Yes, they was Knock Down Punks, but they was never used. They was in storage for many years and was to be replacement punks when the Hit The Kittens punks wore out, but that never happened. They's canvas bodies last a long, long time, 'specially because hardly no one could throw good enough to hit 'em. These poor fellas you see around you was second stringers, the backups. They never got the chance to show what they could do 'cause the Kittens never wore out. The punks sat the bench for many years, in reserve, stuck in a barrel, just waitin' fer a chance to show they stuff, a chance they never got. Idora Park closed before these punks could get the opportunity to perform on stage. They spent many wasted years packed in straw in storage barrels under the Heidelberg Gardens building.

ME: I remember the punks at Idora. They looked just like punks, only they were cats. No, Kittens!

OL: (smiling) Yes, I see that you're a bit slow, but you're catching on. Remind me to put a star on your forehead. Do you even know what the Heidelberg was?

Nice, now the hag wants to be a comedian.

ME: Yes, the Heidelberg was the oldest building on Idora, built in 1898. It had many uses during its' years. It was a dance hall, a roller rink, a bowling alley, a dining facility and in the last few years it was a saloon. It lay vacant for two years after Idora closed and it burned down in a suspicious fire in 1986. So, these ChipPunks were stored under the Heidelberg, but someone must have bought them at Idora's auction in 1984, right? Everything was sold off.

OL: Nope, not everything. The punks stayed in those barrels of straw in the Heidelberg's lower cellar. No one went in that lower cellar 'cause no one knew it was there. The barrels stayed down there with the punks packed inside. They wasn't ChipPunks then. They was just punks, lifeless punks. They didn't ripen until the chipmunks moved in during the cold winter to hibernate in the straw packing. Something happened in those barrels though. Maybe it was chipmunk-punk hanky-panky, maybe it was something in the chemicals in the straw or in the barrels, or in the DNA make-up of the punks themselves. But things changed in those barrels and those punks fermented and took on a life of they own. They come alive, like chipmunks, but kept their punk bodies. That's how ChipPunks was created. Maybe it's evolution, but I like to believe it's God's work.

I glanced over at a nearby ChipPunk with "666" on his body and decided to keep my mouth shut about the God comment. I had my doubts. Was that guy Lucifer? I would be sure to keep a close eye on 666, the old lady and the rest of these critters.

ME: But, how come they didn't burn in the 1986 fire that took out the Heidelberg? How did they survive the smoke and flames?

OL: And there ya are bein' stupid again. Fire burns upward friend, that's where the oxygen is, not underground. The ChipPunks was well below the fire, so the smoke and fire never bothered 'em, it just took away the Heidelberg above. Their secret lair is intact and well-hidden.

Uh oh! If it's a secret, why is she telling us? She doesn't know us, why would she tell us a secret – any secret? The bad feeling I had, was getting worse. Was she telling us the ChipPunk secrets because she intended to do us grave harm? After all, three can keep a secret so long as two are dead… Old lady, Nuck and me… that's three!

ME: So, these things really are alive, and they have a secret nest? Why are you telling us this if it's such a big secret? Do you plan on doing something harmful to us?

OL: Oh no, the ChipPunks don't want to hurt you. Neither do I. They want your help.

ME: Help? How?

OL: There's an evil one among them. She's got a plan to lead the ChipPunks astray. Her plan ain't gonna work, but she's obsessed. She worships a false idol!

I looked over again at the ChipPunk with the 666 on its' body and tilted my head in its' direction so that the Old Lady would catch my drift…

ME: (whispering) Yep, that one, right? He's got the mark of the Beast, literally. Maybe it's not safe to be talking in front of BeetleJuice over there?

OL: Oh no, not 666. Don't judge a ChipPunk by its' cover. He just looks mean. He's sweet as a button.

ME: A button? Really? 666 is a good guy hunh? You sure?

OL: The evil one is an original Kitten from the Hit The Kittens

game. She's the lone survivor of that bunch. She's got a real catty attitude because she was left behind when the rest of the game was auctioned off in '84. The winning bidder tossed her aside 'cause she had ink scribblin' on her body. I guess they figured she weren't perfect because of that tattoo. She's held a grudge ever since.

ME: How can that be? That game was a couple of hundred yards away from where you say the ChipPunks were stored under the Heidelberg building. How did a Kitten punk end up with the ChipPunks?

OL: The ChipPunks move about. They found her discarded in one of the old game buildings by the Penny Arcade and brought her to their secret lair under the Heidelberg. They placed her in a straw barrel and waited… A boy chipmunk showed up and well, she fermented. You can figure out the rest.

ME: Look lady, its' been a really long day already and we just fought one battle. I don't think this is something we'd be interested in. We're tired, sweaty, Nuck's still got grasshopper spit on his face…

OL: There's an Idora Park artifact in it for you if yer successful.

ME: (skeptical) What? Seriously? There's nothing left here. What artifact? We just took the water fountain; the Last Man Standing. There's something else?

OL: Oh yes, the false idol that the Kitten worships is a Bat, a Bat from one of the old scary dark rides, the Kooky Castle. The Bat used to drop down when a ride car would come through and…

NUCKED!

ME: (interrupting) Scare the riders! Yes, I remember the Bat! The individual cars followed a track and special effects would light up to scare the riders. The Bat was one of those special effects, called ballyhoo. It would light up and drop down from the ceiling to scare the riders. The Bat is here? Where?

OL: Oh, there's more than just the Bat, she's got a whole unholy shrine. The drop-down Bat sits on a throne. On that throne is the design of a skull with a Bat body on it and she has a tall tower that looks like it came outta some medieval castle. Like I said, she's got an unholy shrine for that Bat. She must be stopped. Before I tell you more, I need to have your word that you'll help the ChipPunks.

ME: What is it you expect me to do, hit her with a baseball? I never liked baseball. Baseball bores me.

OL: I'm not talking about playing baseball with her, dummy. I'm talking about putting a hit on a Hit The Kitten! Knock the stuffing right out of her, literally!

ME: Well, we're not killing anything, but maybe we can come up with some resolution that benefits the ChipPunks and the Kitten. And if we do this, Nuck and me, we get the Bat?

OL: And the throne and the tower too. That is, if you want them. But you have to make the Kitten problem disappear. Uh, you got a cigarette? I'd kill for a cig right now.

ME: Sorry, don't smoke, never have. Those things will kill you. You're sure this Kitten can't be won over with kindness? You know, maybe a saucer of 2% milk or a fresh litter box? How about a scratching post, a catnip mouse on a string, or we could shine a red dot on the wall and let her chase it? Cats love that stuff.

OL: She ain't that kind of cat, none of that means squat to this angry pussy.

ME: Wait, we're still talking about the Kitten, right?

Okay, so maybe I just said the wrong thing, or it was somehow taken wrong because the old lady glared at me, and I sensed the mood around me change. The ChipPunks all suddenly started in as if on cue with a new chant. It was the song I'd been warned about by the old lady. There began a rustling in the weeds all around me. The ChipPunks were slowly moving closer to me. I think they were angry. Their song was familiar, but no longer a benign children's song. Now it was a cruel variation of a delightful children's tune. Yep, they were angry.

CHIPPUNKS: (singing in unison) My Little Pony, I'd like to kill it, it poops all over the yard!

They kept repeating the same line over and over as they moved closer. I thought, what a horrible thing they did to that gentle song! How terrible! Killing My Little Pony just because it pooped on their yard? I mean, I know it's their war-chant, but what sick mind thinks these things up? First it was twisting the song Little Bunny Foo Foo, by making the bunny bite off field mice heads, now they want to kill My Little Pony because it poops? What's next, Rudolph the Red Nosed Cheeseburger? Mary Ate a Little Lamb Chop? Old MacDonald Ran a Sweat Shop? This was nuts! But back to reality, the ChipPunks were coming after me and I needed to think fast.

ME: Okay, okay lady! Count me in! I'll get rid of the Kitten for you! Now please, call off your sock monkeys!

She nodded at the ChipPunks, shook her head "no" to cease their advance. They obeyed and slid back aways a bit.

OL: Wise move Fred Astaire. So, what's your plan?

ME: My plan? Lady, I just learned about this! What's your plan?

OL: We need to reconnoiter the lair. The Kitten leaves early every morning to hunt for fish at the stream in Mill Creek Park. She's precise. She leaves at 7:00 a.m., fishes, eats, then suns herself in the grass. She's back to her shrine at 8:00 a.m. You be back here at 6:30 a.m. tomorrow to watch.

I was thinking that here was my escape. I could just agree with her, say I'd be back at 6:30 a.m., then just leave, and not come back. But that means maybe never coming back to Idora Park. It also meant I wouldn't get the Kooky Castle Bat and the other stuff that the old lady mentioned. I made up my mind that I would return. Before I could say so, the old lady spoke again.

OL: (matter of fact-like) We'll see you here at 6:30 a.m. tomorrow, this here spot. Bring me a large cup of hot coffee, two sugars, no milk and a double toasted multigrain bagel with cream cheese. Oh, and 666 is going home with you to make sure you get back here on time. 6:30 a.m. – sharp!

Wonderful. 666, the devil himself was going to be my houseguest. I didn't like that one bit and I started to protest, but I noticed that some of the ChipPunks started leaning forward as if to start moving my way or singing "My Little Pony" again. I took the hint. The old lady's words weren't a request, but a demand. The ChipPunks backed off when they saw my shoulders droop. They sensed my surrender.

666 rode on my truck's console. One side of him faced me and the other side faced Nuck in the front passenger seat, keeping his eyes on both of us, a new slant on the phrase two-faced. 666 didn't say anything during the 10-mile drive to Canfield. When we got home 666 hopped out of the truck and headed for the door at the side of my house. He waited for me to get to the door and open it for him. He couldn't reach the door handle (snicker). He hopped toward the kitchen, ahead of me as if he knew the place. I was just about to warn Spike that we have an unusual visitor when I heard her scream. I should have been quicker.

SPIKE: (screaming) A RAT! There's a rat in the house!

ME: (calming her) It's okay, it's not a rat or a mouse. It's just kind of a chipmunk thing.

SPIKE: (apprehensive, holding a broom for protection) A chipmunk? Wearing a sweater? What did you bring home this time?

I explained the whole story of the day's events: the battle with the Big Uglies, the old lady, the barrel of punks, the horny chipmunks, the Kitten, and so on. I introduced 666 as our house guest for the evening, but he just stood there and nodded. As usual, Spike shook her head and rolled her eyes.

It was time to go to work, to formulate a plan for taking out the Kitten. Nuck and I pulled up chairs and started discussing the problem. 666 hopped onto our kitchen island and silently stood there. Once again, the untrusting two-faced thing had one side of his body turned toward me, the other toward Nuck, watching us both. His presence was unnerving, but what could I do? I knew it was fruitless to go elsewhere or ask him to leave. He wasn't going anywhere.

NUCK: Maybe we bring flamethrower, burn Kitten?

ME: You have a flamethrower? Because I don't.

NUCK: No flamethrower, maybe water cannon?

ME: We don't have a water cannon. Besides, I don't want to hurt the thing.

NUCK: Maybe we get boy cat or boy chipmunk for Kitten?

ME: There's already plenty of those on the Idora lands. I think she'd have met Mr. Right by now.

NUCK: Fish trap.

ME: Fish trap?

NUCK: Kitten like fish in stream! Take trap to stream, put fish in trap, Kitten go in trap for fish, trap slam shut. Kitten stuck in trap!

ME: Brilliant, maybe! That might work! But what do we do with the Kitten once we catch her?

NUCK: Uncle Bill Amey love cat! Give him Kitten!

ME: Yes, he does love cats, but Aunt Jean will kill him. I'm surprised she hasn't already done that. The woman is a saint.

NUCK: She put up with everything he do. Collect 100 guitar, she say okay. 10 cat, she say okay! New Jeep, she say get me one too! One more cat, she never notice! Uncle Bill happy, Aunt Jean not kill him. Kitten happy in new home, we get Bat, everyone happy.

ME: (contemplating) I think you're right. Aunt Jean would have killed Uncle Bill by now. He'll weather this one too! I think it's a good plan. Let's get one of those safety traps and a tin of sardines.

NUCKED!

We're gonna catch us a Kitten! Uncle Bill always needs another cat anyway.

I thought I detected a slight grin of approval from 666. Nuck said he saw it too - on the other side of 666's two-sided face.

The next day I showed up at Idora Park at 6:25 am. I'd rather be early than late. The old lady was already there and so were some of the ChipPunks. Nuck and 666 jumped out of the truck and followed me to where the old lady was waiting. I handed her the coffee and held out the bag containing her bagel.

OL: (smiling) You're early! And you brought my coffee and bagel! How sweet! I hope the coffee was stirred clockwise, dredged, stirred counterclockwise and re-dredged?

ME: (confused) What? Counter what?

OL: Didn't I tell you? I like my coffee stirred clockwise, dredged, stirred again counterclockwise, then re-dredged.

ME: (feeling unappreciated) Look lady, the donut place people put the sugar in your coffee. I didn't stir anything, not counterclockwise, not clockwise, not upside down, not shaken and I didn't dredge it either. What the heck is dredge?

OL: What's dredge? Today is another stupid day for you? Dredging is using the spoon to pull the coffee ingredients up from the bottom of the cup to distribute those ingredients, in this case the sugar, evenly within the coffee. You do this AFTER briskly stirring clockwise and again after stirring counterclockwise.

ME: (reaching into the bagel bag) Here, it's a spoon. Stir and dredge all you like.

I heard the weeds rustle and expected to hear that disgusting rendition of the My Little Pony song again, but the old lady gave the ChipPunks her little head shake signal that meant back off.

ME: Touchy little things, aren't they?

OL: (smiling) They care about me. You, not so much.

I handed her the bagel bag.

ME: Can we get down to business now? We have a plan for getting rid of the Kitten. We're going to capture her with some bait and a trap. She won't be hurt. We're going to re-home her with a real softy cat lover. This Kitten is going to live a life of happiness and luxury for the rest of however many lives a Hit The Kitten has. I brought the trap and a can of sardines. 666 listened in on our plan and seemed to approve, but he doesn't say much. Cat got his tongue?

OL: (chuckling) Oh, so now you're a comedian, eh? Cat got his tongue! Ha!

The old lady kept hackling at my joke and motioned for Nuck and me to follow her to the former site of the Heidelberg Gardens building. We took our time getting there to make sure the Kitten had time to go on her daily ritual to the stream to catch her fish and sunbathe.

We took the long way so the Kitten wouldn't see us, over the old picnic area, then across the upper Midway, toward where the Helter Skelter Bumper Car building once sat, then through the brush behind the Fun House site and over to the Heidelberg. There was a stairway at the northwest corner of the old foundation that was completely obstructed by trees, brush and weeds. The stairway led to a deep basement. Once we got to the bottom of the stairs, I pulled out my trusty little flashlight and turned it on. It's tiny, but when that switch is flipped, you'd think the sun just came on. The whole basement was illuminated, and we saw the Kitten's shrine, just as the old lady described it!

The Kooky Castle Bat was there all right! Its throne was none other than a genuine but beat up Kooky Castle Car. The tower that the old lady described was a Kooky Castle Tower from the Kooky Castle building. A hat trick! Three Idora Park artifacts in one fell swoop… er, after we catch the Kitten that is. A deal is a deal, after all.

Capturing the Kitten would take place the next morning. Today was strictly a reconnaissance mission. Now that we knew the layout and lair of the Kitten, we needed to vacate the area before she returned, then the old lady could take us to where the Kitten does her fishing and napping. We'd set the trap today and with luck the Kitten would spring the trap next morning.

Nuck picked up the trap. I carried the sardine tin. The old lady led the way. She was nimble for an old lady. She walked briskly across the Midway, up a small hill, down a bigger hill, through some weeds, along a narrow path, then ducked through a break in Idora's perimeter fence. Just on the other side of the fence was Mill Creek Park land. Another 100 yards and we were at the stream where the Kitten liked to fish. We didn't want the safety trap looking too obvious, so we covered the top of it with a burlap sack and pulled up some branches and leaves to throw on top of the burlap. The contraption looked like a small hill, not at all like a trap. I opened the sardine tin and the sweet aroma of sardines in mustard filled my nostrils. I resisted the urge to eat one. How could the Kitten resist these choice morsels?

I opened the safety trap door, slid the open sardine tin to the rear of the trap, then set the contraption that triggers the door to slam shut when the Kitten goes after the sardines. The noise from the door slamming shut and the realization of her entrapment are sure to startle her, but she won't be injured. And besides, she'll be going to a nice cushy, loving forever home where she'll be spoiled.

Once we were satisfied with the trap and its placement, we headed back to Idora Park. We said our goodbyes in the same spot where we first met the old lady. She handed me the bagel bag and her empty coffee cup and said she'd like the same order tomorrow morning at 7:15 a.m. sharp. I rolled my eyes and took her trash. 666 jumped in the truck and assumed his position on the console again, one face watching me, the other face watching Nuck.

When we got home, I opened the door so 666 could get inside, but I yelled out to Spike right away that the sweater wearing rat was in the house. 666 turned to look at me, but I didn't notice any change to his expression. Maybe the other side of his face smirked? The evening was uneventful except that 666 kept flipping through TV channels. I don't know what show he was looking for, but he never seemed to find it so he just kept flipping through the channels. Spike and I finally went to bed while Nuck and 666 stayed up and watched the TV channels flip. A bonding moment, maybe?

I was up at 6:00 a.m. and after showering I stepped out into the living room and Nuck was asleep on the couch with 666 laying on his chest. I didn't want to know how or what may have transpired that caused that scene. I faked clearing my throat which sounded more like a cough and Nuck woke up at the sound. A quick glass of orange juice and we were out the door and into my truck, 666 on his console perch, watching us both, but not quite sitting in the middle of the console this time. He was scooted closer to Nuck. I guess they bonded last night after all, but I don't want to know any more.

We headed to the donut place to get the queen her coffee with two sugars and toasted multi-grain bagel with cream cheese. I made sure there was a spoon in the bagel bag. She can stir and dredge her coffee exactly how she likes it. Not my job.

We reached our meeting point at 7:13 a.m. and old lady was there waiting, with some of the ChipPunks. She took the coffee and bagel bag, reached inside the bag, and took the spoon. I didn't get a thank you this time.

OL: (between gulps of coffee and bagel bites) Well, are we ready for our morning jaunt to see what might or might not be in your trap?

It was a rhetorical question. Of course, we were going to the trap. I answered any way.

ME: Lead on!

We got to the trap and sure enough, the door was shut. But would the Kitten be inside, or did we capture something else, maybe a groundhog or a raccoon?

NUCKED!

Nuck reached down, grabbed a corner of the burlap sack and pulled it quickly, as if something in the trap might reach up and bite him if he didn't move fast enough.

The Kitten was in the trap. She didn't look too happy about being in there, but she also wasn't going crazy in an effort to get out. All the sardines were gone from the tin, so at least she'd eaten. The Kitten didn't look menacing at all. The way old lady had talked, this cute little thing was mean and nasty. Nuck reached down to put a finger through one of the trap's little openings, to pet the Kitten.

OL: (yelling) LOOK OUT DUMMY! YOU'LL LOSE THAT FINGER!

But that didn't happen. In fact, the Kitten leaned into Nuck's finger, welcoming his caress, rubbing her canvas body against his finger for more human contact. This Kitten didn't seem mean after all. What gives? Was the old lady lying about the Kitten all along? If so, why?

OL: Hmmm, seems like the Kitten likes your pal. Maybe she will be happier living with humans instead of the ChipPunks. I know she always felt out of place, like she was the black sheep of the flock.

That's when everything changed and the weeds around us moved, the hair on the back of my neck stood up and the threatening chant started, "My Little Pony…"

But I had prepared for just this scenario.

Call me untrusting and suspicious, but I had a feeling that a double-cross could be in the making. So, my pocket contained a secret weapon, concealed and smuggled should the contingency arrive. I reached in and raised it high, turning in a complete circle so all the ChipPunks could see. I heard their mass exodus through the weeds, panicked, tripping and scrambling all over themselves to get away from their mortal enemy, the baseball.

ME: (baseball in hand, arm raised high, shouting) YOU SEE THIS, YOU LITTLE RATS?! THIS IS MY KNUCKLEBALL! YOU WANT A PIECE OF ME? WELL, BRING IT ON!

Not one ChipPunk stirred, and everything went quiet.

Then, I turned to look at the old lady.

ME: What's going on here? We had a deal! Why were they chanting? They should be singing something happy since the Kitten is leaving, like maybe sing Twinkle Twinkle Little Star, or Baa Baa Black Sheep. Ummm, okay wait, maybe not Baa Baa Black Sheep…

OL: The ChipPunks wanted to be sure you're taking her away for good. The My Little Pony song was an incentive for you. There's no reneging on our deal, friend.

ME: An incentive? You mean a threat! I've got a good home picked out for her. I told you that. She's going to love it there.

The old lady knew I was extremely disappointed in her. I gently picked up the trap with the Kitten still inside and Nuck and I walked back to the truck to drive Kitten to her new home.

We set Kitten in a picnic basket right outside my Uncle Bill & Aunt Jean's front door. We rang the doorbell and ran. That was weeks ago. Lately I've been seeing my uncle's Facebook posts with a happy Kitten playing and being cuddled in her new home. Kitten is happy, Uncle Bill is happy, and Aunt Jean hasn't killed him. All is good.

Bill and Jean Amey with their new kitten

As for Nuck and me, we retrieved all three of the Kooky Castle artifacts and started refurbishing and restoring them with the help of Mr. Joe Sander and his team of high school students at the Mahoning County Career and Technical

NUCKED!

Center (MCCTC). The artifacts are in The Idora Park Experience collection right now.

We never saw the old lady again and never learned her name, never asked. Nuck and I still wander and explore the old Idora Park property but haven't seen the ChipPunks again. They are very good at staying hidden. Occasionally, though, some creature will scurry through the underbrush, and I wonder if it was a ChipPunk, but it's always too quick for us to catch a glimpse. And, of course, when I'm there I always carry a baseball, just in case.

SPIKE'S SIDE OF THE STORY

Admit it, we were right. If you didn't read the Introduction, this made no sense at all. And if you haven't read the first "NUCKED!", you're wondering what the heck is going on with this craziness and who in the world is Nuck. The good news is, you're going to learn more about Nuck, our 3'-3" knucklehead ninja and how he came into our lives in the next chapter, "The Narcissist and the Knucklehead". Hint: Nuck is short for Knucklehead. And the title "NUCKED!" comes from all the times we've been… well… you know… NUCKED! by Nuck.

But for now, let's get to Spike's Side of the Story, otherwise known as the truth, about how we really got the Kooky Castle Tower, Bat, Sign and Car… and of course, the Punks and Kitten.

One of the most common things we get asked about is how we find Idora Park artifacts that have been in hiding for 30 plus years. And the short answer is, through all of you.

We've created a network and that network has grown

exponentially through the years. In 2014 we had about 2,000 followers on The Idora Park Experience Facebook Page, and we thought THAT was amazing. As we write this, we have crossed over 20,000 followers and we simply find it hard to believe.

That so many people would think what we do and write about is worthy of their time is humbling to us. And we're very grateful for every one of you.

One of the side benefits to having such a loyal and dedicated following is they love helping us find new things. Sometimes it's just a clue, or something they heard, or maybe saw once, long ago. But often those little clues turn into gold for us.

The Kooky Castle coup is one of those wins.

It was in the early days of creating the museum and opening it to the public that we began to hear stories about several different Idora Park artifacts. A handful of people talked about how, several years ago, Idora Park items were used as props for a haunted hayfield ride at a nearby farm. The stories varied, as they always do, but there was a common theme: castle and bat.

Jim knew it had to be the Kooky Castle. And then one day, it happened. A friend said they knew who had purchased the Kooky Castle artifacts at the auction... would we like the contact information? Of course!!!

A phone call later we'd learned that indeed this was the person who had purchased the Kooky Castle artifacts at the auction. Unfortunately, they had sold them to a farm to be used as props for a haunted hayride. They couldn't remember for sure which one, but knew it was no longer in operation.

And then one day a good friend said, "You know the Kooky Castle Towers are right around the corner from you in that corn field."

WHAT??? Right around the corner from us?! Yep!

We jumped in the truck and raced the one mile to the corn field. Jim completely ignored the stop sign as he made the right turn off

Turner Road onto Kirk Road and then fish-tailed the rear-end of the truck as he made the right turn into the driveway of the owner of the corn field. I nearly went through the windshield when he slammed on the brakes and skidded to a halt, throwing the shifter into park.

When this man wants something, not much is going to stand in his way.

He swung open the door and jumped out... well almost, he'd forgotten to unbuckle his seatbelt and got clotheslined in the rush. Grumble, grumble, curse, curse...

Regaining his composure, he looked around to see if there was anyone watching or any hidden cameras recording what was surely a social media worthy comedy video clip. When he had checked all angles and knew his antics were free from public embarrassment, he ran like lighting up the steps to the house and began banging on the door.

"What the...!?" The corn field owner grumbled as he answered the door.

Jim, never one to waste time on small talk blurts out, "Do you have Idora Park stuff?".

Jim could barely contain his excitement as he waited for him to nod in the affirmative and share where the scary goods might be hiding.

Okay, so maybe it didn't happen quite like that. Hey, who said Spike's Side of the Story was the whole truth and nothing but the truth? I only ever said I'd tell you the truth... I never promised not to dress it up a little. Besides, I need to have some fun every now and again too.

You see, my memory isn't as good as it used to be... but don't tell Jim, he's still afraid of it, very afraid. I don't want to lose that edge with him. So exactly who said what to whom when, well...

It's all kind of blurry now. Several people told us about the haunted hayride. And Jim did talk to the person that bought most of the Kooky Castle stuff at the auction who said he'd sold it to a farm.

NUCKED!

A good friend is the one who said it was in the corn field about a mile from our home. So, you see, most of this is true... even if we can't remember the exact dates, people and places.

But I assure you Jim is a very safe driver and would never intentionally break the law by driving through a stop sign or fish-tailing his pretty truck. Although if you read the first "NUCKED!" you know he would steal a bunch of abandoned artifacts if I'd let him... I guess that's a Youngstown thing... (I'm telling you; you should have read the other book!)

With the information from the former owner of the artifacts and our friend, Jim made a few calls, set a date and to the farm we went.

As for the corn field owner, well he was just as nice as could be. He told us how we should just drive back to the corn field and see what we could find... and if we could get it out of the field, we could have it. A DONATION no less!

And that's what we did. We drove back through the trees to the now dormant corn field. There we found several Kooky Castle towers hidden behind trees and brush. Only one was in good enough shape and in a position that we could retrieve it safely.

Jim carefully removed the brush from around it and gingerly pulled it up onto our trailer. Yes, he brought the trailer... just in case we got lucky... And we did!

We stopped to show the owner what we had and to make sure that it truly was okay to take it. It was!

CORN FIELD OWNER: "Oh, by the way, I have the Bat from the Kooky Castle too. Do you want to see it?"

A little while later and a few dollars lighter (he wanted a small fee for the Bat) and we were on our way home with some cool artifacts.

We now had a Tower and a Bat from the Kooky Castle ride, but we didn't have a Kooky Castle car...

That would come later when we would make a deal with an individual who had a Kooky Castle car rotting away on their property. It took some time, talking and money but eventually we had the car to go with everything else. And Jim got him to include a "Keep Arms & Legs inside Car" sign that was part of the ride too.

The Tower, Bat and Car were all in very bad shape, but they were home, and we would ensure they had a long life ahead of them.

And the Punks and Kitten? Well, we bought them online. No funny or scary story… See, isn't Jim's story telling much more fun?

But the story doesn't end there…

L-R Joe Sander and Steve Vesey ("WFMJ Today" news anchor)

LIFE LESSON: The right partner is everything

We've dedicated this book to Joe Sander, Collision Repair Instructor at the Mahoning County Career and Technical Center (MCCTC). Joe and his teams of students and colleagues at MCCTC have been a godsend to The Idora Park Experience. They have collaborated with us on seven different projects and every one of them has culminated in an amazing, finished product, several of which you will read about in this book.

The Kooky Castle Car and the Tower were both projects done by Joe and his teams. The car was completed by the class of 2019 – 2020 and the Tower was completed by the class of 2022 – 2023.

But it wasn't easy finding Joe… Until it was.

In 2013 when we retired and moved to Canfield and began construction of The Idora Park Experience, Jim had the idea to approach MCCTC and ask if any of their programs would be interested in working with us and helping with the restoration of some of the artifacts. We thought it was a no-brainer to work with the local trade school and involve the students in an historically relevant project and at the same time, help to preserve the artifacts. We were willing to pay for all the supplies and help with the oversight of the projects.

Jim contacted the dean of the school at the time and made his pitch. He was promptly told that they don't do that kind of thing.

Okay. It was just an idea. We thought it was a pretty good idea. But we were obviously wrong. But as always, you don't know until you ask.

Fast forward a couple of years. We're having a yard sale that we set up by The Idora Park Experience building. Jim has a 1963 Ford Econoline van parked in the driveway near the building and it catches the eye of a passerby.

Joe Sander was his name and over a friendly conversation about the Econoline that morphed into a conversation about The Idora Park Experience, Joe drops that he is an instructor for the Auto Collision Repair Program at MCCTC, and he would love for his students to work on restoring one of these artifacts.

Wait? What?

"But Joe, your guy said you don't do that kind of stuff."

"You talked to the wrong guy! He doesn't make those decisions I do."

The next day Joe stopped by to discuss what artifact they would do first.

The collaboration between Joe Sander's class and The Idora Park Experience has become somewhat of a community program with local news outlets doing stories about the projects each year.

Often, when we do public appearances, former students will show up with friends and family members. They'll check to see if we brought whatever project they were a part of, and then proudly introduce their companions and talk about their experience working on the project.

It's an incredible feeling to think that you may have positively influenced the life of a child and we hope we have.

We couldn't be more pleased with their work or honored to be partners with Joe Sander and MCCTC. It is our dream that one day, long in the future, that the students who have worked on these projects will walk through a museum with their children or grandchildren and be able to say… I did that! Only time will tell.

While MCCTC administration may not have originally wanted to be part of this, we have no doubt that what Joe and his students have done in collaboration with The Idora Park Experience has given MCCTC and their career-oriented programs more visibility in the community and promoted the trades as a viable option for high school students who are trying to figure out what comes next.

Thank you, Joe!

THE NARCISSIST AND THE KNUCKLEHEAD

I have no idea how Spike is going to tell her side of the story on this one because everything you're about to read is true. Well, maybe there's a smidgen of embellishment, but not much. Names have been changed to keep me from being sued.

This is how we started collecting the Idora Park "Big Stuff".

Sometime around 2005 I started looking for larger Idora Park artifacts. I wanted something bigger than the occasional ashtray or poster that I'd find on eBay or in a yard sale when we'd come home to visit family in Ohio. Spike and I were living in Chantilly, Virginia, then. I worked in Washington, DC.

Although living in Virginia, I started putting ads in all the local newspapers in and around Youngstown and on the amusement park and carnival ride websites, looking for that "bigger" Idora Park artifact, like a rollercoaster car from the Wildcat or Jack Rabbit.

I heard nothing for months. One day while on break from teaching a class in Washington, D.C., my cell phone rang. The screen showed "Blocked Caller ID". I answered the phone anyway.

UNKNOWN MALE CALLER: (whispering) I know a guy who has some stuff you're looking for.

I figured, "wrong number". Is this guy a drug dealer?

ME: I think you've got the wrong number.

CALLER: No, you're the guy looking for Idora Park stuff, right? Big stuff. I know a guy who has big stuff from Idora.

ME: (excited) Oh, yeah, sorry. I thought you were a drug deal… Er, never mind. What kind of big stuff? Who is the guy and how do I reach him?

CALLER: His name is Oswald and he's an odd ball, but he collects cool stuff and some of it is from Idora. He's in Bubalini, Ohio. He has a Wildcat car and other big stuff. But be wary. Don't trust him. He'll screw you over in a heartbeat. Oh, and don't tell him I gave you his number.

(Yes, he gave me Oswald's phone number.)

ME: (puzzled) Well, I can't tell him who you are because I don't know who you are. Your caller ID is blocked. Where's Bubalini in Ohio? I never heard of It.

"CLICK" He hung up.

I called the number that the mystery caller gave me. It was a landline, not a cell phone. A recording that I presumed to be Oswald's voice was on an answering machine telling me that I should have called his cell phone because he never answers his home phone. His recorded voice had a tinge of rudeness and impatience to it, as if it was a chore just to be bothered to make the recording. But he did state his cell phone number in the message.

So, I dialed it next. Well, I didn't actually dial, like with a rotary phone. I tapped out the numbers on my cell phone. Again, I received a voicemail recording telling me that he wasn't available right now, but as a last resort I could call his home phone, but he never answers that phone or checks those messages. I could also leave a message on his cell phone, and he'd get back to me. It felt like I was playing phone tag with myself.

I left a message on his cell phone telling him my name and that I'd like to talk to him about some of his Idora Park collection. Then, I waited.

Two weeks went by and no return call. I called the cell phone again and left another message. No return call. I began calling every week or so, leaving roughly the same message. After a couple of months, I actually got through and he answered the phone.

ME: Hi, Oswald? I've left you a few messages about your Idora Park collection.

OSWALD: (wary, suspicious, rude) Yeah, what do you want?

ME: I've been collecting small Idora Park things for a few years now, but I'm looking for something big, like maybe a Wildcat car.

OSWALD: Who gave you my number?

ME: I don't know. Some guy with blocked caller ID called and gave it to me.

OSWALD: Yeah, but who was it?

ME: He wouldn't say his name and his number was blocked.

OSWALD: Probably brother Chet. He'd do something like that.

ME: Your brother? As I said, I don't know who it was. He didn't say.

OSWALD: Well, he's not my real brother. He's not even my "friend brother" anymore because he ripped me off. Now there's only three of us "friend brothers" because I unbrothered brother Chet. There used to be four of us, now there's only three.

How do I respond to this? "Friend brothers"? "Unbrothered"? The guy is definitely strange.

ME: I have no idea if it was your brother Chet or someone else. He didn't tell me his name.

OSWALD: (agitated, correcting me) I told you, he's NOT brother Chet anymore. He's just Chet.

I was trying to figure out how to keep this guy talking, how to relate to him in his own "language". I could tell that the communication could go south and end at any time. I couldn't let that happen if he had larger items from Idora. Time to don kid gloves if I was to make any progress. The guy was definitely self-centered. Welcome to Oswald's planet.

ME: Like I said, I don't know who called. He didn't give his name.

OSWALD: Well, I have some Idora stuff, but I don't sell. I like to think of myself as "Mr. Idora", you know. If I did sell, I'd have to get good money out of it. You got good money?

ME: (puzzled) What's "good" money mean?

OSWALD: Not cheap. I'd have to get at least what I paid for the stuff.

ME: Fair enough, I guess. When can I look?

OSWALD: I don't know you. Let me get to know you and we'll see.

ME: How am I supposed to do that? I live in northern Virginia. I'm six hours away. I can't just meet you any time. How about next weekend? I can drive up to Ohio and meet you then.

OSWALD: I'm busy Sunday with brother Horace. He's one of the three brothers. There's only three of us now. Chet is definitely out! Can you be here Saturday at 11:00 a.m.? I don't get up before 10:00.

ME: Great! Thanks! I'll be there. I just need the address.

OSWALD (with a stern warning) The worst thing you can do is be late. Brother Horace was late once, and he almost became unbrothered. My time is important.

ME: It's a six-hour drive from Washington, D.C. If there are no traffic delays, I'll be there on time.

Oswald gave me the address, said it was the only houseboat on the street and then he hung up on me.

THE NARCISSIST AND THE KNUCKLEHEAD

Who is this self-centered jerk, I wondered. Houseboat on the street?

I couldn't wait for Saturday to come…

I wanted to leave Friday, but Spike and I had to work. Trying to drive anywhere near Washington, D.C. during the after-work rush hour, especially on a Friday, is long and torturous.

So, Spike and I left our Virginia home at 3:00 a.m. Saturday for the six-hour drive to Bubalini, Ohio. The distance was 306 miles to Oswald's house, er… houseboat. This gave us seven hours to make the five-and-a-half-hour drive, plenty of time to get there by the agreed upon 11:00 a.m.

Unfortunately, we didn't make it on time to Oswald's house. We got there 10 minutes late.

Tragically, some fella had decided to take his life on Pennsylvania Route 76. He'd been traveling west on Rt. 76, parked his car on the shoulder of the highway, got out of his car and waited until a semi-truck was coming, then he walked right out into the truck's path. The truck driver couldn't stop. We didn't witness this firsthand, thank God. But we saw the aftermath.

Traffic was stopped on Rt. 76 as police and EMTs responded and investigated. When Spike and I were finally able to see what was causing the traffic delay we saw a body lying on the ground with a tarp over it. The left arm stuck out from under the tarp. I didn't know this person, but I felt a sense of loss for his life and anyone who knew and loved him. Something terrible happened in that person's life and he just felt that it was too much with which to cope. It is so heartbreaking.

I tried to stop thinking about the accident and the death, but the thoughts lingered and still do, these many years later.

I needed to get to Ohio on time and we were going to be late no matter how fast I drove. We made it to Oswald's house at 11:10 a.m., 10 minutes late. An extremely gaunt looking white male, age about 65 stood in the driveway looking at his wristwatch in a very dramatic way, passive aggressively letting me know that I was late, and he wasn't happy about it. As we pulled closer to where he stood, I could see a mop of thick red hair that didn't quite fit with his chronological age. As I went to introduce myself, I saw why, the hair didn't fit. It was a very bad hairpiece, and it was crooked on his head.

For the next 17 years that I associated with Oswald I noticed that as he grew older the hairpiece remained red, crooked and younger than him.

Someone, whom I presumed to be Oswald's significant other stood nearby, a small woman wearing Muslim garb. She was covered in black clothing from head to toe. I was surprised to see though, that her eyes were not covered as traditional Muslim garb required.

I said hello to her(?) and received acknowledgement with a head nod in return.

OSWALD: (perturbed) I said don't be late and you're late. My time is important.

ME: It couldn't be helped. It's a 300-mile trip and traffic was stopped on Rt. 76 for almost two hours because of an accident.

OSWALD: It can ALWAYS be helped. You should have left home earlier.

I bit my lip to suppress my anger. I knew then, standing there in the year 2005, that no explanation would be good enough for Oswald because in those few words and actions of his I had already figured him out. Nothing mattered to Oswald, but Oswald himself. This planet Earth belongs to Oswald. The rest of us are here to do his bidding. For the next 17 years Oswald would prove this to me again and again.

The black-clad woman stood nearby but wasn't introduced. I was unsure if it was okay or not okay to converse with her, so I said nothing else. Something about the way this person moved had me wondering, "it" didn't move like a woman. Was it male?

THE NARCISSIST AND THE KNUCKLEHEAD

Then, I saw the houseboat! Oswald lived in a beat-up old houseboat! How did the city allow a houseboat, a dilapidated one at that, to be placed on his property? How did it even get here?

Oswald's front yard had old, animated characters from an amusement park or miniature golf course surrounding the place. I'd seen such things before, but his collection was dingy and dirty. Some were cracked and broken. There were also a couple of old coin operated kiddie rides in similar condition, faded paint and dirty. Background music was playing, the kind of music that you'd typically hear in an amusement park kiddie land. It wasn't current music, like you'd hear today. It was older stuff, from the 1950s and 60s. Spike and I just looked at each other like, "What the heck is going on here?"

A large old building was in the back yard. It had to be at least 60 feet long by 40 feet wide. Alongside the building were more coin operated kiddie rides and parts of amusement park rides in the yard. Everything looked rough, neglected, weather beaten. I discovered that this was a regular theme with Oswald, he took care of nothing that he owned.

We went inside the building. It was two-stories tall, and the first floor was packed, stacked to the ceiling and walls with old pinball machines, claw machines, money changers, jukeboxes, parts of carnival rides and more stuff. I was in amazement. We had to maneuver through little pathways in the cluttered walkways, climbing over and around machines, toys, junk.

Oswald led us to a far corner and pointed at a pile of old stuffed toys and pinball parts piled on top of something bulky and painted orange.

OSWALD: There's a Wildcat car under there. I want what I got in it, $1,500 good money.

I found out years later that he'd paid $300 for that Wildcat car.

I looked at Spike. She nodded her agreement to the stated price.

NUCKED!

ME: I'll take it. How do we get it out of here? It's packed in tight. We'd have to move everything out of the way.

OSWALD: I have a guy who does that. Do you want to see a Jack Rabbit car?

ME: (excited) Yes, of course!

We hacked our way back out of the jungle of stuff and headed outside. Around the back of the building sat two old roller coaster cars in deteriorating condition. I recognized one of the cars immediately. It had a tall weed-tree growing through the front seat, a Jack Rabbit car from Idora Park!

OSWALD: Same price, what I paid. $1,500, good money.

Again, I found out later that Oswald had actually "taken" this Jack Rabbit car from the Idora Park property when the deteriorated rollercoaster structure was torn down in 2001. Is "stolen" too harsh a word?

I didn't haggle. I agreed to Oswald's price on both cars, all "good money" of course. I felt that the coaster cars were in the wrong place at the wrong time, and I couldn't bear to leave them there. I walked over to the Jack Rabbit car and grabbed that weed-tree thing, yanked it by the roots out of the front seat and threw it in Oswald's yard.

That was our first trip to Oswald's home, but there would be many, many more visits over the coming years. I sensed that he had other Idora Park secrets that he wasn't prepared to reveal and over the following years I was proven right.

Before we left Oswald's he said he'd have the coaster cars ready for pick-up the following weekend, but he'd like the $3,000 in "good money" immediately. I paid him half and told him he'd get the remainder when I picked up the coaster cars. He didn't like that, but that's all I was willing to do and he reluctantly relented.

Spike went back to wait in the car while I gave Oswald his down payment. I bid goodbye to Oswald, and I walked back to our car and climbed into the driver's seat. Spike was already in the front passenger seat. I could tell by experience that she did not care for Oswald one iota. But then, neither did I.

A year later I would buy four old Arcade machines from Oswald, paying him $4,800. When I went to pick up the machines, he had re-sold two of those machines to someone else. It took eight years before he partially repaid me. Amazingly, Oswald demanded that I place a plaque bearing the inscription "From the Collection of Oswald" on the artifacts that I purchased from him. He became extremely angry when I told him that this would never happen. Donating is one thing and worthy of a plaque or donation card, but selling is another animal altogether. Oswald doesn't see the difference. This is his planet, after all.

Anyway, …

I heard a crunching sound coming from the car's back seat so I turned to look. The little, black-clothed person I saw earlier was strapped into a child's car seat back there, only it wasn't a woman like I'd thought. The mask was off, and the person was male! He was eating from a bag of Frito's corn chips.

ME: (startled, looking at Spike and the stranger) Um, what's going on here?

SPIKE: (matter of fact-like) He said he works for you now. He's hungry so I gave him Frito's. It's all I had in the car. I guess he likes them.

ME: (shocked) What? Who is he? Why is he in the car? I have no idea who this is.

LITTLE PERSON: My name Puddintame. Ask again I tell you same!

ME: (frowning, confused) Yeah, sure it is. That's ridiculous. That's a child's game. I remember it from when I was a kid. What's your real name smart alec and why are you in my car? How did you get a car seat in here?

LITTLE PERSON: My name Puddintame. Member in good standing, Amalgamated Union, Baker and Ninja, Local 867. Pudding

my bake specialty, so union name me Puddintame. Ask me again…

ME: Yes, I know, you'll "tell me the same." So, you're a baker in a union… with ninjas? How's that work?

LITTLE PERSON/PUDDINTAME: No, I ninja in union with baker and more ninja. Long story. I 'splain later. Now I work for you, boss. You call me Puddin'.

ME: Uh, no. You don't work for me and even if you did, I'm not calling you Puddin'. And don't call me boss. I'm not your boss. Now, get out of my car and go back to Oswald where you belong.

LITTLE PERSON/PUDDINTAME: Don't know him, don't trust him. First time here, like you. I come here for you.

ME: (looking at Spike) This makes no sense. He doesn't know me. Why would he be here for me? He couldn't have known we were coming here. Aren't you going to say something to him? He needs to go home or back to his bakery or something. He can't stay with us.

SPIKE: (shrugging, looking me in the eye) This is your call. He wants YOU so YOU decide what to do.

ME: (to Puddintame) Look, you don't work for me. We don't know each other. I can be a real pain in the neck. You wouldn't like me. I don't even like me most times. I don't know what I'd do with a ninja anyway. I have no work for you. What do you even do, just bake?

LITTLE PERSON/PUDDINTAME: I help you find many Idora Park thing.

ME: I don't want to find many Idora Park things. I'm content now. I've found everything I wanted to find, a coaster car from each of the two big rollercoasters. There's nothing else I need.

THE NARCISSIST AND THE KNUCKLEHEAD

LITTLE PERSON/PUDDINTAME: (shaking his head) You wrong. You not stop. I know this. You on mission, quest! You just not know it yet. Oh, I ask you, why you call wife "Spike"? She pretty. She wear spike heel?

ME: (surprised) WHAT? Spike heels? What kind of question is that? It's none of your business why I call her Spike! And you're wrong about a "mission". I'm not on any mission or a quest for anything. Now, get out of my car!

He didn't put up an argument. I watched him unstrap himself from his car seat, step out of the car, remove the car seat and step away from the car. I was relieved. I started the car, put it in reverse and looked over my shoulder to back out of Oswald's driveway. I glanced to the front of the car at Puddintame as he stood there watching us back away. He put that black mask over his head again. I felt sorry for the poor thing, but what am I going to do with a pudding baking ninja?

I looked out the rear-view mirror to guide the car backward until I reached the end of Oswald's driveway, then looked to where Puddintame was standing. He was gone. I asked Spike where he went. She said, "I don't know, he just sort of vanished!"

Hmmm, maybe he's got some ninja skills too? Spike and I talked about Oswald and Puddintame as we drove to Canfield, Ohio. We'd bought a home there just a few months earlier. Our plan was to retire early, sell the Virginia home and settle in Canfield, near family.

We pulled into the driveway of our new home and got out of the car. We immediately got an unexpected surprise. Puddintame was sprawled out, face down, clinging to the roof of the car!

ME: (incredulous) Are you crazy? How did you get up there without us seeing you? And why? Do you realize how dangerous that was? What if you had fallen off? You could have been killed! Even worse, if a cop had seen you, I would have gotten a ticket!

PUDDINTAME: (calmly) Ninja Style Point for roof ride. You sign training sheet, maybe I get promotion!

ME: What? Style points? Promotion? That's nuts! And why do you speak in broken English?

PUDDINTAME: Style point help ninja promotion. I speak like all ninja speak, like movie ninja.

We stood there at the car, just Spike, me and this little baker-ninja, looking at each other and wondering what to do with him.

ME: (shaking my head) Listen Puddintame…

PUDDINTAME: (cutting me off) Boss, Puddintame temporary name. I stay with you and Spike now. Union rule say YOU choose permanent name. Puddintame kaput now. I work for you. You choose new name!

ME: Look, don't call me boss. I don't know what's weirder, you or your union. I'm not giving you a permanent name and I'm not calling you Puddintame or Puddin' either. What a knucklehead!

PUDDINTAME: (looking at me, head tilted) "Knucklehead". I like name.

ME: (sternly) No, that's not a name and it wasn't a compliment.

SPIKE: (interjecting) Uh, no! That's not a nice name. But I have an idea. How about we shorten "Knucklehead" to just "Nuck". How's that sound? Nuck!

I stood there, frowning at the little guy while Spike was talking. This wasn't what I wanted. Puddintame mentioned a "mission" about Idora Park "stuff". But I'd just completed my "mission" and got the "stuff" I'd wanted, the two coaster cars. There was no mission, no quest. The search was over. The scary thing though, was that Spike appeared to be softening her demeanor about "keeping" him. I was ready to put a stop to it, to tell him to hop in the car and I'd drop him off somewhere.

But then, the little guy reached out his hand to Spike and she took it, with no hesitation. His face showed relief and gratitude, like a great worry of some kind had been lifted from his mind. His shoulders straightened and he seemed a little taller, as if a heavy weight had just left his body. But there was more, like in the flash of just an instant, I thought that maybe this feels right, maybe it's the right thing to do. Maybe we don't need him, but he needs us, that he's supposed to be with us for some reason. Only time would tell.

I followed behind Spike and "Nuck" as they walked toward our home. He looked up at her and said, "I happy now. I make clothespin cookie. You have ingredient?"

SPIKE: (smiling) Yes, I think so. But we can run to the store for anything you might need. It's funny that you bring up clothespin cookies, that's my husband's favorite!

NUCK: (nodding and smiling) I already know this.

I guess we have a ninja or maybe he has us. And his name is Nuck.

SPIKE'S SIDE OF THE STORY

Jim's right. True story. Well… Almost… The names and places were changed just like he said… but if you know… you know.

Excuse me for a moment while I go call our attorney. I need to find out if we can get sued for telling the truth.

LIFE LESSON: Welcome life's inspirations

Narcissists and other obnoxious people aside, life is full of inspiration and most of the time it shows up when you least expect it. You just have to be open to it.

Nuck was an inspiration for us.

People ask us how Nuck came about and why a Ninja. I honestly don't know if there is a clear answer to either question.

Early in our endeavors to get the big stuff it seemed like our missions never went smoothly. If there was a way to get lost, to meet a stranger than normal stranger along the way, or to break, lose or forget something, we did it.

And, of course, neither of US could be to blame!

Which sometimes made things worse.

You know how it seems like some people must have a guardian angel looking after them and helping them through life? Well, that's not us, we haven't really led guardian angel worthy lives. But a menace causing ninja who stealthily swoops in and wreaks havoc when you least expect it, well that's more our style.

Being able to point the finger at some mysterious invisible guy messing with our best laid plans made the difficulty much more bearable and helped us to get past the frustrations to solutions quicker. And gave us something to talk about on some of those very long boring rides.

Knucklehead is a term of endearment Jim uses for our children and grandchildren when they do something silly. So, when it came time to give our little friend his own identity, it was only natural that we'd choose the one that had been living with us for so many years… Knucklehead… Nuck for short. If you read the first "Nucked!" you know that we have more than one ninja… we also have Buck aka "Buckethead", which is also a family term of endearment used when someone does something empty headed.

And just as the knuckleheads and bucketheads of our family are very dearly loved, so are Nuck and Buck. They have become very real to us. They travel on our adventures with us, bring levity to difficult situations when needed, and are the root of very much laughter and even more story telling.

Nuck was the spark that ignited Jim's over-active imagination into high gear and put into motion the creative and funny as hell story telling he's been doing for over a decade.

Nuck and Buck work in tandem to keep us on our toes and always moving forward. Especially when we most just want to quit.

We're both very thankful for this little bit of Life's Inspiration and we know that if our fans knew just how very much Nuck is behind all that we've accomplished with The Idora Park Experience, they'd love him as much as we do.

THE BIG "O"

We're going to time travel. This story is taking you back to the year 2012, two years before The Idora Park Experience would open for the first time.

Look closely at this photo. It's one of a pair of large magnetic signs that I was going to stick on the sides of my truck to help me commit a crime. I don't own a business named RWE nor do I work for a business named RWE. Notice anything wrong with the sign? No? Look at the spelling of "Lampost". It's missing a letter "p". Yep, it's supposed to say "Lamppost". Two p's, not one!

How am I to pull off a heist if the sign on my truck is misspelled? A misspelled sign would be a clue to an observant citizen or police officer that something fishy might be going on and worthy of investigation. Simple mistakes can trip up an otherwise well-planned operation. For example, look at the Watergate break-in. A piece of tape on a door lock was found by an observant security guard and it started a domino effect that ended up bringing down a U.S. President.

So, what crime would I be committing?

Let me explain.

I contacted the church that owns the Idora Park property and offered a $$$$ donation if they'd let me "rescue" the lamppost located just inside the park as you came in the Billingsgate entrance off Canfield Road. It was broken and rusted and dangerously close to falling apart.

I waited for their response. And waited… and waited.

I knew it wouldn't be long before parts fell off the lamppost, became a hazard to trespassers, and then went the way of the many other Idora Park lampposts… scrapped.

More of our history gone, but not if I can help it.

I was getting that lamppost one way or another!

My $$$$ offer to the church included the coveted big Green Globe. The Green Globe was probably three feet around, a big round metal cube with a light bulb in it, shining down. I learned from, Lenny Cavalier, one of Idora Park's previous owners, that the Green Globe was a leftover from a car dealership job. An electrician installed big globes at a car dealership parking lot and had one spare, so he offered it to Idora. And, here it was, decades later, after the devastating 1984 fire, still standing high above where Idora Park's office had once sat. That fire caused Idora Park amusement park to close forever, but the Green Globe survived and still stood, decades before the fire and another 28 years after the fire.

That Green Globe has been called a bunch of different names... the Green Globe, the office globe, the round light above the office, the shroud of Idora... maybe I made that one up. Anyway, I had to have it!

If you walked onto the Idora Park property you couldn't miss the Green Globe. It sat high in the air atop a tall steel pole.

Lots of people wanted that Green Globe for their Idora Park collection.

It became the "holy grail" of Idora Park, a most prized possession for any collector of Idora Park artifacts. It's so recognizable that anyone who sees it will know what it was and where it was located, assuming they'd been to Idora Park, of course.

It was an icon.

I decided to do more than just talk about getting this Green Globe.

I planned to TAKE it.

Legally, of course, unless I had to resort to other means.

I've always tried to be a 'do-er' not a talker and I just HAD to get the Green Globe!

I came up with two plans to get the Green Globe as well as the Idora lamppost on Billingsgate Road.

One plan legal, one not so much.

Plan #1 - Buy it. If that failed, go to Plan #2...

Plan #2 - Steal it! Create a fake electrical company, buy hard hats, a matching safety vest and magnetic signs for my truck. I even had fake business cards made and fake license plates!

I used the name and phone number of a real electrical company, RWE, in the far-off state of Oregon, hence the letter "O" in the address. There really is a Salem Oregon.

Anyone (Ohio police) who saw the magnetic signs could be fooled into thinking that RWE from Salem O is nearby Salem Ohio, not far away Salem Oregon.

NUCKED!

I even used RWE's real 1-800 phone number and planned the "job" for a Sunday. You see, RWE in Oregon is closed on Sundays, plus their time zone is three hours behind Ohio. Anyone suspicious enough to check up on my "activities" by calling RWE would get their answering machine, since the business is closed on Sunday!

Genius!

I imagined this scenario; I'm at the Idora Park property unbolting the tall pole that holds up the Green Globe, my truck with RWE magnet signs sits nearby. I'm wearing my safety vest and hardhat when a cop pulls up and asks me what I'm doing. I give him one of my fake business cards and tell him I'm removing the Green Globe

for restoration (not exactly a lie). The cop is a little suspicious as all cops should be. He calls "my company", RWE to verify. Cop gets the answering machine message, "Sorry, we're closed on Sundays!"

I look at the cop after he gets off the phone and I say, "Yeah, the corporate suits get weekends off. Shlubs like you and me, we gotta work weekends and holidays. What can we do?"

Cop nods, we both shrug. He gets it. He's right there with me, working on a Sunday. He and I are two ships passing in the night. Well, daylight actually. Cop takes off, heads for Donutland. I get back to work on those bolts…

A great plan! Foolproof, unless you put a knucklehead ninja in charge of ordering the magnetic signs for the truck and business cards and he can't spell "LAMPPOST"! Plan #2 was scratched.

What am I supposed to tell the cop, "Hey, we're electricians, we can't spell too good!"?

Sheesh!

Back to Plan #1, the legal one (and crossed fingers).

A rep of the church finally contacted me, and we met at the Idora Park Parkview entrance. It was a Saturday. Parkview was once the main entrance to Idora Park. There's still a fence around the entire Idora Park property and a gate at both entrances, one on Parkview, the other gate is way across the park on a road named Billingsgate. The last standing lamppost is just inside the Billingsgate entrance. The Green Globe is located at about the midway point between the Parkview entrance and the Billingsgate entrance.

Church guy unlocked the Parkview gate, and I led him toward the Green Globe's location to show him exactly what I was talking about.

We walked, looked, walked some more... where the heck was the Green Globe?

How could I be in the wrong spot? I knew exactly where to find it, but it was nowhere in the skyline... I stood where the office had been, searching the sky for the Green Globe.

A terrible, sick feeling hit me, a realization that the Green Globe was gone! I forced myself to look away from the sky, to look at the ground. A light pole was laying on the ground! Oh no, no way... it was the Green Globe's light pole!

I ran through some brush and weeds to the spot where the globe should be at the top of where the pole lay in the weeds. No Green Globe! I searched all around for traces of the Green Globe... nothing. A thief! Some dirty rotten good for nothing thief had stolen the holy grail! I was furious! Furious with myself for not stealing the Green Globe before the thief got it and furious with Nuck for his bad spelling that disrupted my plan to steal the thing.

I ran back over to the light pole and saw that someone had unbolted it at the base... that's how they got the Green Globe.

They let it fall! Idiots!

The Green Globe was probably destroyed, but most certainly it was badly damaged. I could tell because of the way the pole fell and where the Green Globe would have struck the ground. Oh, the humanity!

I knew it was my fault, really.

Like a dummy I had posted on my personal Facebook page that I was returning from Washington, DC to get the Billingsgate lamppost and the Green Globe. (Back in 2012 Spike and I lived just outside of Washington, DC. We didn't move back to the Youngstown area until a year later, 2013.)

Someone must have read my Facebook post and acted before I could claim the Green Globe.

I was torn between admiring that someone had the guts to do such a thing and being angry that it was gone and probably my fault because of my Facebook post!

I looked at the church guy and shook my head. I told him it was my fault.

He said, "Do you want the pole?"

Seriously? Did he really just ask me if I wanted the pole? The pole!

I bit back the words that I wanted to scream. Instead, I kept cool, just shook my head, no. What am I going to do with the pole? That's like getting the stick that the lollipop came with, but not the lollipop.

I finally came out of my daze and went into a panic as I remembered the Billingsgate lamppost! What if the thief got that too?

Oh no! I took off running toward its direction! Ever seen a 54-year-old man run when he hasn't run for a long, long time?

It ain't pretty, but that's okay, it doesn't last long.

I felt the concrete in my legs after about 50 yards (okay, maybe it was 10 yards).

I reached a clearance in the weeds and could see from a distance that the Billingsgate lamppost still stood!

I swear that I could hear our National Anthem playing in my ears… it was the part, "… and so proudly we hailed, at the twilight's last gleaming. And the rocket's red glare, the bombs bursting in air, gave proof through the night, that our lamppost was still there!"

Then again, it might just have been the echo of the 12:00 o'clock emergency siren that blares out every Saturday. I wasn't exactly sure.

I felt the rush of pride and looked back at the church guy.

I pointed in the direction of the lamppost and said, "I'll take it down tomorrow!"

As church guy and I walked back to the Parkview entrance I looked over at the Bus Canopy… hmmmm…

I said to church guy, "How much for that bus canopy?"

He told me I could have it since the Green Globe was missing.

But I knew that one day that Green Globe would surface.

Fast forward two years to the Grand Opening Weekend at The Idora Park Experience, April 26, 2014 – the 30th anniversary of the fire that ended Idora Park.

We have two-thirds of that Parkview Bus Canopy.

Thieves again! They got the other one-third thanks to an electrical storm that stopped me from picking it up after I took it down to the ground.

One-third of the Idora Park Bus Canopy is erected in The Idora Park Experience building. If you were here April 26 & 27, 2014 you walked right under it! We've since moved it inside, and it proudly houses the 18' handcrafted wooden model of the Wildcat roller coaster that John Kondas built. We also have the last standing lamppost (with two pp's) that was on Billingsgate Road.

Uh, back to the story…

NUCKED!

It was opening day, Saturday, April 26, 2014, when "SHE" walked up to me inside The Idora Park Experience and said, "I don't know if you'd be interested, but I have this big round green light from Idora… "

I excitedly cut her off, "Show me with your arms, how big?"

She reached up and made a big circle above her head, a big "O"! I looked around to make sure no one heard us. There might be other Idora Park treasure hunters about. I pulled her to one side.

I was so excited! I felt like a junkie meeting his pimp. No, pimp is the wrong word. I meant drug dealer, a junkie meeting his drug dealer.

She told me that the Green Globe was smashed up and broken in two, and she was planning to use it as a planter in her garden. What?! A planter? That's almost blasphemous!

Lady… no! I need to see it!

The next day, Sunday, April 27, she returned and led me to her car.

She opened the back door, and I peeked inside. There, laying across the back seat, the twisted and broken aluminum body of the Green Globe! I removed the pieces and placed them on the ground in front of me.

I looked at the lady, "Don't even tell me who did this. I don't want to know. How much do you want for it?"

The deal was made (after a near clash with Spike) and with some help I carried the twisted broken pieces of the Green Globe into The Idora Park Experience building.

We set her on the floor, and I felt that rush of pride and satisfaction…

I can rebuild it. And I did.

Oh, uh… I need to call church guy about getting that pole after all!

Gee, I hope no one steals that too!

SPIKE'S SIDE OF THE STORY

First, let me say that the first words I ever heard Jim Amey say were "I always knew I'd end up on one side of the law or the other." He was a law enforcement officer in the U.S. Air Force at the time, so I was pretty convinced I knew what side he'd chosen.

I'm not so sure anymore…

And second, a more appropriate title for this chapter would have been "The S#!* We Had to Buy Twice".

Seriously!

Jim would have you believe that the Green Globe lady was a walk down easy street. He made this deal sound like he was the king of making deals and all he had to do was ask Miss Green Globe, "How much do you want for it?", and with that, the deal was done.

Not so fast kiddos.

That's not quite the way it happened.

Let's back up and set the stage for what was really happening. Remember early in the story when Jim explained that he paid the church for the Green Globe? And then… when he met 'church guy'… he found out the Green Globe had been stolen?

Yeah, let that sink in for a minute. WE BOUGHT AND PAID for it. But it was STOLEN before we could take possession of it.

Now, fast-forward to The Idora Park Experience Grand Opening… Miss Tight Jeans sashays away (she's in the first NUCKED!), and while Jim is still mesmerized by the view, in walks Miss Green Globe…

By this time, I'm paying attention… very close attention… I mean I used to look good in my jeans too, so I know exactly what's going on in that man's head! And I know it doesn't have anything to do with making good decisions, business or otherwise. Yep, my wifey spidey senses are in full alert mode.

So, on Sunday, when Miss Green Globe comes back into his life and Jim has this look like someone just offered him Cadbury's chocolate and hot tea, you can bet your life I followed him when he followed her.

I walk up to the two of them standing just a little too close to each other… and looking like they were going to climb into the backseat of her car together… and I hear her say, "Well, how much will you give me for it?"

WTH???!!!

I could see the panic in Jim's eyes when he looked over her shoulder and saw me standing there.

JIM: (stuttering just a bit too much) Eh, oh h-h-hey S-S-S-Spike. What'r you doing here? I mean… don't you have some shirts to sell or something else you need to be doing right now?

ME: (just as sugary as I could muster) I just thought I'd check to see if you needed help with anything. What's up?

JIM: (pointing to the backseat of her car) Uhhh, w-w-well y-you s-see… we're just talking about the Green Globe. Remember the Green Globe. She's got it. See it?

ME: The Green Globe? Oh… I thought… uh… never mind. So, this is the globe that was stolen. This is great! We got it back.

JIM: Uh, not yet. But we're talking about that.

ME: Oh, so what's the issue?

JIM: She wants to sell it to us.

ME: (looking at Miss Green Globe) Oh? For how much?

MISS GREEN GLOBE: Well, what'll you give me for it?

I could see the reflection of the mushroom cloud in Jim's eyes when my thermo-nuclear explosion happened.

ME: (in a tone indicating I'd had enough of these shenanigans) We don't play that game! We already bought and paid for that thing once… you are in possession of stolen property… OUR stolen property. If I called Canfield police right now, you'd be arrested for being in possession of OUR stolen property! So, I suggest that if you want to sell it, you tell Jim how much you want for it. And then he can agree or not. But we won't be playing the "what will you give me for it?" game.

Seriously folks, when you go to the grocery store, does the grocer ask you how much you will give for a gallon of milk, dozen eggs, or loaf of bread? NO! They are all clearly marked with a price. And if you are buying a house or a car, the seller doesn't ask you what you're willing to "give for it". They put a price on it. If you don't like it, you can make a counteroffer or go somewhere else and try to get to a better deal.

I can't tell you the number of times people with Idora artifacts have said to us "What'll you give me for it?" It drives me crazy. What I hear is "I have no idea what it's worth, but I want all of your money for it."

I just snapped.

With that, Miss Green Globe immediately named her price. Jim agreed to it almost before she uttered the words. And then, and only then, was the deal done.

NUCKED!

I have no doubt that she took less than she wanted, and he paid more than he wanted (and certainly more than I wanted). But isn't that the basis of every good deal?

And yes, we paid for the Idora Park Green Globe twice.

Jim lovingly repaired and restored it and now it's a working lamp in The Idora Park Experience.

LIFE LESSON: Be firm... AND fair

Whether it's in business, daily living, partnering, or parenting, there eventually comes a time when you have to draw the line. The challenge is always to find that sweet spot that makes everyone happy and yet also hurts everyone just a little.

No, we shouldn't have had to pay for the Green Globe twice. However, we really wanted it... well, Jim did...

And Miss Green Globe had it.

It was simple supply and demand.

Rest assured, had her price been unfair, we would have walked away (well I might have been dragging Jim by his ear... and I might have called the police while doing so...) but we would have walked.

We've done it with several deals (the walking away, not the calling the police part), and I can honestly say that with the exception of one or two situations, we've never regretted it. And in some cases, we were able to come back later and make an even better deal – with some items even being donated, or with deals that we all left feeling really good about.

In the few cases that things didn't work out so well, we can honestly look ourselves in the mirror and know that we did our best to be firm AND fair.

THE ELEPHANT ESCAPADE

NUCK: (excited) Boss, Lost River Elephant in New York! Friend tell me!

ME: (unimpressed) What? It's not in New York. I know exactly where it is and so do you. The owners don't want to part with it. You already knew that!

NUCK: Yes, boss! This one not Idora. This one New York. Lost River Elephant like Idora! For sale!

ME: (excited) You're kidding, right? You found a Lost River Elephant? A real one? Do you know how rare those are?

NUCK: Not real elephant! Lost River Elephant, fake.

ME: (eyes rolling) I didn't mean "alive", I meant "genuine", as in a genuine Lost River Elephant! Not many of those were made and very few survived. If you found one that makes only two that I know of, Idora's and your discovery. They were made by a company called

"Messmore & Damon". The elephant is made of fiberglass with an electric motor and mechanical parts that move the elephant's head, neck, trunk, ears and tail.

The Lost River Elephants were all named "Jumbo". The company made lots of different animatronics, even huge dinosaurs. They started their business sometime around 1914 or 1916. Messmore died in 1961 and Damon died in 1962. A brilliant dark ride creator named Bill Tracy used the Messmore & Damon elephants to create the Lost River rides at several amusement parks. Idora Park was one of those amusement parks.

NUCK: (interrupting) Bill Tracy, detective! Comic book hero!

ME: Uh no, that was Dick Tracy, knucklehead. I'm talking about a real person, Bill Tracy, no relation to Dick Tracy the comic strip guy. Bill Tracy created amusement park scary dark rides all over the country. He changed Idora Park's Rapids water ride into the Lost River in 1968 and converted the Fun House into the Whacky Shack that same year. He also created Idora's Gold Nugget western ride in 1963.

NUCK: (stifling a yawn) Boss, I here about elephant, not history lesson. You bore everyone sometime.

ME: Hmmm. Right, so where in New York is this Lost River Elephant?

NUCK: Town called Blimpf. Way north. Friend find it. He call me, tell me!

ME: I'll look it up and we'll do the GPS thing. So, does your friend own this elephant? Can we work out a deal? What's your friend's name?

NUCK: Elephant in auction. Online auction. You bid. Friend name Bongo Jerry, drummer. He work with elephant, play bongo drum while elephant wiggle head, ear, tail, raise trunk.

ME: (confused) ugh, an auction? I hate auctions. Stuff tends to go high, and this elephant is rare. There's probably going to be a lot of interested bidders. So, your friend Bongo Jerry, what kind of gig is that, to play drums all day and night next to an animatronic elephant? That seems like an awfully monotonous job.

NUCK: We talk Bongo Jerry later, talk elephant auction now. No one bid, boss. Auction start last month, one week left. Still no bid!

ME: (excited) That's great news! A month in and no bids. But that could mean that interested parties are waiting until near the end to bid. That's called "sniping". So, have you got some photos of this beauty?

NUCK: (apprehensive) Elephant ugly. Sit outside many year, 30 year. He broke, dirty, ugly.

Nuck pulled out his tablet and went to the auction website to show me the photos. He was being kind when he said the elephant was ugly. It was a mess. The thing stood in an overgrown field of weeds, one of several elephants in the auction. The others were not animatronics, not Lost River Elephants. They were stationary statues. I couldn't tell if they were made of concrete or fiberglass.

The fabric that covered Jumbo's neck joint was torn, and the area of the mouth showed a large, rotted section of wood and machinery hanging from it. Jumbo's ears were bent, torn and sagging and his tail was gone. There's supposed to be an access panel on the elephant's side that allows entry to the motor, gearbox and mechanicals that operate the trunk, ears, head and tail.

That access panel was missing, leaving the elephant's internal workings open to rain, snow, insects and other creatures for the past 30 plus years. Someone had even stuck Jumbo's broken off tusks in the opening. The thing that bothered me the most though, was Jumbo's bowed head. I know it's not a real elephant, but he looked as though his "spirit" was broken, like he was lost and forgotten and had given up hope. Crazy to think that way about an inanimate thing, I know. But I do.

Jumbo obviously had had a very rough life standing in that field alone for three decades. We needed to change that. We needed to win the auction and get him to lift that proud head again. Oh, and waggle those ears, lift that trunk and wiggle that tail. We had a mission! But it sure looked like a lot of work and a lot of money was going to be needed IF we could win the auction.

ME: (puzzled) Nuck, the color of Jumbo's "skin" looks blue! He's supposed to be grey.

NUCK: (shrugging) It November, boss. Maybe he cold?

ME: You just triggered a thought. It's November, late November. The auction doesn't end for another week! Jumbo is in upstate New York, over 500 miles away. If we win this auction we might have to drive through snow, towing Jumbo on a trailer. I wonder, how heavy is Jumbo? Can we even lift him to get him on a trailer? Does the auctioneer have equipment for loading an elephant for us? And, since he's in a field, what do we do if the ground is too wet to get a forklift or something to pick him up?

NUCK: (reassuring me) Boss, no help from auction people. I already check. But we figure out. We always figure out. Most always. Baker Ninja union already know. Cheap labor. You win auction, union rescue Jumbo!

ME: (smiling) You're right! We'll figure it out. We just need to win the auction, then worry about getting Jumbo loaded up and home. So, you already talked to your union, eh?

NUCK: (nodding and smiling) Four union member on standby!

ME: Great, that makes six of us! We should be able to lift a fiberglass elephant onto a trailer, right? Will your buddy Bongo Jerry help?

NUCK: (ignoring or evading my question) We grab leg each, one person take head, I lift tail…

ME: (interrupting) His tail is missing. And you couldn't reach it if there was a tail. That elephant is over eight feet tall and you're barely three feet tall. I guess your job will be taking photos. By the way, how reliable are your union pals? Do you know them?

NUCK: Two baker, two ninja. Baker Cory, baker Terry, ninja Paul, ninja John. Spike go too! She take photo!

ME: Those don't sound like code names. Are you sure the two bakers are up to the task? What about your buddy, Bongo Jerry, maybe he can help?

NUCK: (reassuring me) Not ordinary baker, boss. Baker first, ninja second. Uh, Bongo Jerry part of auction.

ME: (confused) What do you mean Bongo Jerry is part of the auction, he's the auctioneer?

NUCK: No, boss. Bongo Jerry in auction. He stay with Jumbo.

ME: (even more confused) No way! He can't be part of the auction if he's a person. That's not legal.

NUCK: Bongo Jerry not alive. He like robot, like elephant.

ME: (incredulous) Are you nuts? How can he be a robot? You said he was a friend that contacted you about the elephant. A robot that speaks? Like what, the robot from that old TV series, *Lost In Space*?

NUCK: No, boss. Bongo Jerry play Morse Code on drum, send message that way. I know code, learn about elephant, tell you!

ME: (my head is swimming) I have no idea what you're talking about. There's always something weird going on inside that brain of yours. Now you've got a bongo drum playing robot who communicates with you by Morse Code?

NUCK: Boss, maybe he not robot. More like mannequin.

ME: Seriously? So now your friend is a dummy? You can communicate with a dummy? Why am I not surprised? I guess what they say is true, it takes one to know one.

NUCK: (scolding me) Dummy not nice name.

ME: Get over it. I can't wait to meet your pal, Bongo Dummy. Another thing, I'll never understand how or why there'd be such a thing as a Baker and Ninja union, even though it seems to work for you folks, and you've always come through for us in the past. Your baker guys saved us in "The Big Uglies", the grasshopper war that Spike and I wrote about in our last book. It's still strange though, bakers and ninjas together in the same union.

NUCKED!

(Note to reader – go get the book! It's called "NUCKED! Misadventures with the Idora Park Experience Ninjas")

I watched the auction website every day to see if there was any bid activity on Jumbo. Sure enough, there was a bid of $90 with three days left in the auction. Two people had bid, so there was no telling if the maximum bid was $90, or if the high bidder had bid more and they were only showing the amount by which he or she was beating the other bidder. Frustrating!

But I now knew that there were at least two other persons so far who wanted Jumbo. The stationary elephant auctions were in the $1,000 range and there were a bunch of other amusement park items being auctioned as well. Everything up for auction looked like it had been neglected, sitting in storage either outside or inside for many years. I wasn't interested in anything but Jumbo and maybe Bongo Jerry, whatever that was – robot, mannequin, dummy? He came with the elephant, but there was no mention or photo of him on the auction site.

I was antsy, but not ready to bid. Not yet. I needed to be patient and not alert the other bidders too soon. The bid on Jumbo was still $90 on the last day of the auction. I told Spike that I was going to make a maximum bid of $500. She was fine with that. I prepared to take my sniper shot bid, but I would wait until six seconds before the auction closed, then fire off my snipe bid. Instead of typing in the Spike agreed upon $500 max, I found my fingers inexplicably typing in a bid of $1,325 and hoping that it was way more than enough to win, but I did not hit "enter". I still had about one minute before the auction closed. I prayed, please go cheap so Spike doesn't find out how high I really bid!

I refreshed the auctioneer's page every few seconds. The countdown was killing me. Would my bid be high enough? Is there another sniper with deeper pockets who wants Jumbo even more than me? Who wants a beat-up old elephant anyway? I mean, besides me?

Seconds ticked away like hours… I checked my internet connection, 5G! Nothing was going to stop my bid!

T-Minus 10 seconds until auction end. The seconds ticked away… I was locked and loaded with one chance at this. If my bid wasn't high enough, I wouldn't get a second bid in on time. T-Minus 6 seconds! It's now or never, time to…

FIRE!

I hit "enter" on my computer keyboard, sending my bid racing through the internet like a hellfire missile. It streaked out of my laptop computer, straight and true, up through the atmosphere at the speed of light, ricocheting off some metal satellite in outer space KA-PING, speeding back through the layers of the atmosphere, racing back to America just as fast as it left home, then KA-BLAM!!! Hitting that auctioneer's website like a Mike Tyson uppercut! (I hoped.)

The current high bidder probably never knew what hit him. I imagined him - smugly sitting at his computer screen, wearing his safari outfit, big game hunter style, sipping a Mai Tai cocktail with his feet up on his desk just waiting to bag the elephant, pay his $90 plus auction fees and plan his trip to pick up the elephant.

That just wasn't going to happen! I'll bet that bid of ours knocked the umbrella right out of his drink when he refreshed his computer and saw that he'd been outbid. (Um wait, Mai Tai's have umbrellas in them, right? I'm not much of a drinker. I don't even know what's in a Mai Tai! Anyway, that's what I imagined, a Mai Tai with an umbrella.)

Jumbo just wasn't meant to be – not for Mr. Mai Tai anyway. I hoped.

And then… The auction ended! I needed to refresh the page to find out the result, afraid of what I might see. Did I win? Did my bid even register? Was I outbid? Did my bid even get there in time? I stared at the computer screen, exhaled, took a deep breath, then refreshed the page…

YES!!!

NUCKED!

We did it Spikey! And we got Jumbo cheap! I didn't have to pay $1,325, no siree! With fees I got Jumbo for a measly $130! Yay, $130!!!

Ninjas! I need ninjas. And bakers too! I had to assemble the rescue team and quick. It was late November, and the threat of snow exists for the entire 500-mile trip from Northeast Ohio all the way to Blimpf, New York, and back again on the 500-mile return.

Where exactly the heck is Blimpf, New York, anyway?

Nuck alerted his crew, Cory, Terry, Paul and John, all members in good standing of the Amalgamated Union of Bakers and Ninjas, Local 867. They were to meet us in Blimpf in three days. The bakers, Cory and Terry would be bringing cheese blintzes for everyone. I don't even know what a blintz is, but what a cool word! Blintz! The seven of us set out for the mission, the four union folks, Nuck, Spike and me.

We broke the trip into a two-day drive. The ninjas all went in a motorhome owned by Cory and Paul. Spike and I drove our Jeep and decided to rent a cargo trailer in New York to transport Jumbo and Bongo Jerry home. I figured that a one-way trailer rental would be cheaper than paying for the extra gas it would cost in pulling my own, heavier trailer. Boy, was I wrong.

I called around to find a trailer rental outlet in Blimpf so I could rent a 5 foot by 8 foot open top trailer, then I was going to head to the auction location to meet the ninjas and load Jumbo into the trailer for the trek home. But things went ugly. The rental place was called Uncle Sherman's Trailer Rental, Storage and Deli. The young guy working behind the counter informed me that he was the son of the owner, Uncle Sherman. I read his name tag, "Sherman III".

SHERMAN: I'm sorry, but we can't rent that trailer for a one-way trip. You'll have to rent a covered trailer. The open-top trailers are for local rental only.

ME: (stunned) That's not what I was told over the phone when I reserved the open-top trailer. I was assured that it was fine for a one-way trip.

SHERMAN: Yes, that was a mistake. It's for local rental only, not one-way.

ME: Yeah, you said that. Now what am I supposed to do?

SHERMAN: (smiling) Oh, easy peasy! We'll rent you a closed-top trailer for the same price since it was our mistake.

ME: You've got a closed-top trailer with a roof that's over eight feet tall? Because that's how tall our elephant is, eight feet!

SHERMAN: (shocked) I'm sorry sir, but we can't allow animals in our trailers. They make a mess and none of our enclosed trailers are that tall anyway.

ME: It's not a live elephant, it's fiberglass. He's potty trained. But you don't have a trailer with a roof tall enough to fit him anyway. I knew I should have brought my trailer. It was perfect for Jumbo, but no, I had to try to save money. Sheesh!

I spent the next 10 minutes explaining the elephant situation to Sherman number three.

SHERMAN: (smiling) I have a suggestion! Why don't you do this; rent the open-top trailer, pick up your elephant, bring the elephant here and we'll rent you a storage container for the elephant? When you get home to Ohio you can get your trailer and pick up your elephant! And, when you rent a trailer and a storage space from us you get a free deli sandwich! We have roast beef and baloney.

I noticed Sherman's dirt-greasy hands and nearly gagged at the thought of a sandwich.

ME: Sandwich? Ummm, no thanks! Maybe next time. Rent a storage space? Heck, I really wanted to get Jumbo home right away. Now the cost of a storage space, logistics with the ninjas, ... So, what's a storage space going to cost me?

SHERMAN: (still smiling) Well, the storage space is 8 feet tall by 10 feet wide and 10 feet deep. It'll be $185 per month or any part thereof. So, if you only use the space for…

ME: (interrupting) Yes, yes, I know. It's $185 even if I occupy the space for one day.

SHERMAN: (still smiling) Correct! Would you like to rent a space?

ME: No, but I'm going to anyway.

I paid the fee plus a deposit, then paid for the open-top trailer. Spike and I hooked the trailer to our Jeep and drove to the auction house to meet our help, Jumbo and Bongo Jerry. When we arrived, the bakers and ninjas were waiting.

ME: (surprised at their clothing) Why aren't you guys dressed in your uniforms? I thought you bakers had to wear white jackets and the ninjas had to be dressed in ninja gear! What gives?

NUCK: Boss, union rep in Blimpf angry, say this mission job for Blimpf union, not Ohio union. He report any Ohio baker and ninja in uniform. We get trouble, so no uniform. Blimpf union rep pound sand.

ME: (impressed) Pound sand, eh? Ouch! Do you even know what that means? Never mind. Okay, I appreciate you guys doing this, so we'll keep it hush-hush from your local union and the Blimpf union rep. Pound sand, that's funny, Nuck.

We set off for the auction site and checked in with the auctioneer folks as soon as we arrived. We found Jumbo out in the field of weeds, just like the auction photos showed. He was a mess, even worse in person than in the photos. His fiberglass body was cracked in places, the wood platform inside the body was rotted and falling apart. The same was true of Jumbo's mouth. A large wood platform had fallen from inside Jumbo's head and was hanging from his mouth. That platform supported a motor that operated the elephant's ears.

I peeked inside the opening on Jumbo's left side and noticed an infestation of wasps. Luckily, I'd foreseen this problem and brought along several "bug bombs" which I discharged into Jumbo, then covered the opening with a tarp so that none of the wasps could escape Jumbo's body and attack us. We waited 30 minutes to let the bug bombs do their thing.

Once satisfied that we wouldn't be stung, four of us grabbed an elephant leg each, hoisted Jumbo a few inches off the ground and "walked" him over to and onto the rented trailer. We tied Jumbo down securely in the trailer and departed the field of weeds that had been Jumbo's home for the past 30+ years, then set off for Sherman's storage location in Blimpf, New York. As we began to pull out onto the road I saw him, BONGO JERRY!

Bongo Jerry was a mannequin after all. He was a native, not quite the same size or stature as the bongo playing native that was at Idora Park's Lost River, but a bongo playing native none the less. He looked awesome, dressed in native jungle-like attire with a cool looking vest and a top hat. He had two bongo drums with him. I stopped the Jeep and Nuck and I jumped out to take a look.

ME: (greatly impressed) He's amazing! But how does he communicate with the drums? Is there a power cord or something that makes him work? I'd like to talk to him, find out everything I can about him, what he's seen, where he's been, who created him...

NUCK: (laughing) You funny, boss. I make up story. Ha ha! No Morse Code! He dummy, like you! You say, "I want talk to Jerry, get to know him!" Ha ha! Two big dummy, you and him! Ha!

ME: (embarrassed and a little angry) I should have known better than to believe you. You know, maybe instead of Nuck I should call you "Jerk"!

NUCK: (still laughing, and placing his head close to Jerry's drums as if listening) Jerry what you think? What you say? Wait boss, listen… I think I hear drum! Ha ha ha!

ME: (embarrassed, shaking my head) You know what knucklehead, you had your funny little game, now load your friend Jerry in the trailer with the elephant. It's getting late and I'm hungry.

NUCK: (still leaning close to Bongo Jerry's drums) Say what Jerry? Boss, Jerry say he hungry too, for DRUM STICK! Ha ha ha!

ME: Jerk!

Jumbo stands 8'-3" tall, four feet wide, eight feet long. I know because I measured him. Those extra three inches in Jumbo's height shouldn't be a problem for the 8-foot-tall storage space, right? I mean, how much trouble can three extra inches cause? I found out soon enough.

My plan was that we would tilt Jumbo into the storage space while he was standing up, just enough to clear the 8-foot height of the door opening. Then, once we cleared Jumbo's back under the door, we could lift him and store him in the standing position. That didn't work. The roll-up door on the storage space hung down another four inches. So, instead of eight feet, we had a height of 7'-8" for an 8'-3" elephant. We tried everything, but once we cleared the low hanging door the interior ceiling of the storage space was right at eight feet tall. Jumbo was too tall, by three inches. Unfortunately, we had to lay Jumbo on his right side onto some packing blankets and push him inside the storage space.

We left Jumbo laying there for two weeks, returning in early December to retrieve him. The guy at Sherman's Rentals was kind enough to use their forklift to help us load Jumbo onto my trailer. They offered us free deli sandwiches again, but we declined. We had a long 500-mile trip home from Blimpf, New York. I had Nuck, the comedian with me.

At one point we stopped for gasoline and a guy at the adjacent pump walked around the trailer, staring closely at Jumbo, then asked me while I was filling my tank, "Is that a bison or a buffalo?"

I thought about that for a while. I mean, it looks just like an elephant. Why would he ask if it was a bison or a buffalo? I don't see how anyone can infer that bison and buffalo even look remotely alike. They don't. And neither of them looks like an elephant.

Sure, the elephant on my trailer was a bit beat up, but it had the big ears, the elephant head, bits of the trunk, etc… It was obviously an elephant. Finally, I answered calmly, "Hippopotamus. It's a hippo." He frowned, thought about it for a second, then smiled and said, "Oh, okay! I see that now." I smiled back.

I finished filling the gas tank. The air was cold, and a few snowflakes were falling. I just wanted to get home. We were finally leaving New York and heading into Pennsylvania, then Ohio.

Lots of thumbs up and photos from people passing us in cars and trucks all the way from upstate New York, through Pennsylvania and into Ohio. I'm sure most of those folks never saw anything like us.

Jumbo needed lots of work and again I called on Joe Sander, at MCCTC for help. Joe took the elephant in and began the outer body restoration. Our good friend Larry Cadman helped me repair Jumbo's interior, making the trunk, ears, tail and head move again. Spike made Jumbo's new neck, trunk and tail skins. I made the ears and a new access panel. Patricia Andio, our neighbor across the street supplied us with an actual horsehair tail clipping from one of her horses!

Jumbo the Lost River Elephant is back amongst the living, and he works great. He's not from Idora Park, but he is an original Messmore & Damon Elephant and an original Bill Tracy Lost River prop.

NUCKED!

We put our Jumbo on display with Bongo Jerry on the drums. Okay, so he's not the actual bongo player from Idora Park, but he's ours and we love him. Did you know that Idora's bongo player burned in the April 26, 1984, fire? Yes, sadly. We have photos of him on fire. Sad.

Jumbo and Bongo Jerry complete our Rapids/Lost River collection. They are on display with the only Rapids/Lost River Boat known to exist while the original Idora Park Lost River soundtrack is playing. That soundtrack is courtesy of our friend Joyce Aey. Her late husband Jack was the guy who kept the sounds of Idora Park going for many years. Joyce found his working original tapes after Jack passed away and she graciously donated the collection to us.

We still have our hopes up and our fingers crossed about someday acquiring the original Idora Park Lost River Elephant. Time will tell…Or, maybe Bongo Jerry will.

SPIKE'S SIDE OF THE STORY

I learn entirely too much when I'm reading Jim's stories for the first time. There is a big, very big, difference between $500 and $1,325.

We've long established that Jim has a penchant for taking creative liberties with the truth in his writing. But seriously? That's an $825 swing. This from the guy who has me check gas prices on the internet when we're on road trips so he can fill up the vehicle for three cents fewer a gallon.

For perspective, our motorhome has a 55-gallon tank. If it were empty, which it never is because he won't let it get below a fourth of a tank... but let's just say it's empty... that's only $1.65 difference.

But somehow, I'm not supposed to notice a difference of $825!

Okay, rant over.

Well not quite. Did you catch that this Jumbo is not from Idora Park, but we know where the original one is? Yep! And that with time and a little luck, we might even see Idora Park's in a museum someday.

NUCKED!

So why get a duplicate Jumbo? And one that needs hours and hours (and more than a few dollars) of restoration work… by skilled trades people at that?

Because we can. And because it's an adventure. And because we don't know for sure that we'll see the original Idora Park Elephant ever again. And the people of this community loved the Lost River and deserve to feel as much of that great memory as they can.

These are all good reasons… but $825 worth of good reasons?!?!

Okay, now my rant is over… (well not really, but I'll take it up with Jim later.)

Jim pretty much tells you the truth in this story… and obviously told me more truth than he wanted me to know. There isn't much I can add, other than to say, Nuck getting Jim with the Bongo Jerry doing Morse Code on the Bongos was pretty darn funny.

In all seriousness, Jumbo and Bongo were both projects that were overwhelming at times and downright hilarious at others.

Getting Jumbo out of that field with our team of bakers and ninjas (otherwise known as our good friends Cory Nestor, Paul Clapham, and John and Terry Brennan) and into a trailer, then driving through an upstate New York village and getting him into a storage unit that was way too small for an 8'-3" Elephant was just the start.

Well actually it wasn't. The plan from the beginning was to rent a one-way trailer locally and put Jumbo in storage for a few weeks. We had other commitments and couldn't bring him home immediately.

The problems started when the trailer company didn't have storage and the storage company didn't have a trailer. That should have been our first clue that things weren't going to go as smoothly.

We decided to scope out the storage facility before picking up the trailer. Good thing we did. The narrow gravel driveway leading to the storage units made it impossible for us to get Jumbo where we needed him to be. Luckily, the storage company was used to this

SNAFU and fully refunded our money. But now we needed to find another storage unit… ASAP!

But by this time, we were also running late for picking up our trailer so off to the trailer company we go. Lo and behold when we get there, they advise us that the only trailers they have left are enclosed. What?! So now we not only don't have a storage unit, but we also don't have a trailer.

But as Nuck says, we always figure it out.

Turns out the trailer company has a sister store that isn't officially open yet, but they do have available storage units and some open top trailers available. They just aren't set up for conducting business yet. Can we wait until Monday? Uh, NO!

A quick phone call to the sister company manager and a miracle happens. He'll get us the trailer and the storage unit, at a great price, and worry about charging us when they get their technology up and running! Can you believe it!?

The new store is across town but on the upside, it's closer to Jumbo than the original store. Off we go! Get the trailer, scout the storage unit… it looks big enough, easy access and on pavement! This is going to work!

Well, it wasn't quite that easy… the door to the unit was just a bit shorter than Jumbo so we had to lay him on his side, twist him around and finagle one set of legs in first then the other. But we got him in there!

That was the easy part, we had no idea how we were going to get him out when we return in two weeks.

Luckily, the storage facility manager, who had already saved our butts once, showed up with a forklift and a couple of able-bodied employees and saved our butts again. And with our friend, Larry Cadman's help, we got Jumbo out of storage, locked securely into place on our trailer and home safely.

And that's when the real work began. Again, Joe Sander and his MCCTC team jumped in to help reconstruct Jumbo's body. Larry got to work on the mechanicals and electricals, and I took on getting the ears, neck and tail fabrics replaced.

What was Jim doing you ask? Why, he sat around eating bon bons and telling us what we were all doing wrong. (Okay, he worked a little). The finishing touches came from Keith Sturgeon of Skeeter's Grafix who painted Jumbo's eyes so well that it appears Jumbo is watching you no matter what direction you move, and Joyce Aey who donated the original Lost River sounds.

Keith Sturgeon giving Jumbo his beautiful eyes

And Bongo Jerry? Well, he's a replica that we built. He is truly a mix of whatever parts and pieces we could find in our massive Halloween decorations and props collection.

He has man mannequin parts, lady mannequin parts (should that be ladyquin?), and loose bits and pieces of hands, feet and of course a head. He looked like a patchwork quilt from the movie "Jeepers Creepers" until Jim broke out the spray paint and painted him.

Add a wig, earrings, bracelets, necklace, grass skirt, a nifty vest and cool top hat and eye patch and of course two bongo drums and voila! Bongo Jerry! (The name is ours… a play off the rock band named "Mungo Jerry").

Jerry wasn't complete though. Jim and Larry rigged a motor to the arms and set the range and tempo so that it appears Bongo Jerry is playing the drums to the sounds from Idora Park's Lost River.

Pure genius in action!

It was truly a great project, and it was wonderful, once again, to see so many people with the ability and willingness to step up, bring their talents, skills, time and passion to the table so that Jumbo, Bongo, and everyone else could benefit.

L-R: John Brennan, Jim Amey (hidden), Cory Nester, Terry Brennan, Paul Clapham

LIFE LESSON: Passion is contagious... So is Lunacy

You know it. You've felt it. That energized sensation when you are with someone who is so passionate about something that they can almost make you believe you are too.

It can also make you feel as if you are missing something because you don't feel that same passion and wonder if there is something wrong with you because you don't.

You're not. And there isn't. Passion is an individual thing, and it can be different things to different people.

In the right hands, heart and brain it can be something that accomplishes amazing things. In the wrong ones it can be a cult or gang leader guiding lost sheep down a path of lies and destruction.

Luckily Jim isn't a cult or gang leader and the passion he oozes is shared by many who loved Idora Park. But what happens when that passion catches fire with people who know nothing about Idora Park, or even Youngstown for that matter?

Well, in Jim's case he got a fully staffed Elephant Escapade.

Disguised as a baker and ninja, Cory Nester and Paul Clapham, ran full steam ahead into the Elephant Escapade, not because they love Idora Park… they aren't even from the area. They did it because they were infected by Jim's passionate lunacy.

When Cory and Paul heard we were working out a plan to get Jumbo, they immediately changed their road-trip travel plans and announced they would join us in upstate New York. They were giddy with excitement for their upcoming adventure. I wondered if they really understood what being this close to lunacy… 'er passion is really like.

The best part, Cory and Paul dragged their friends (who are now our very good friends), Terry and John Brennan along with them. In fairness, I don't think Terry and John knew what they were getting into and certainly didn't expect to be identifying as either a baker or a ninja that day, but they took it like champs and worked like the dickens to help us get Jumbo loaded, unloaded and settled into his temporary residence.

When it came time to hit the road to get Jumbo, another victim of Jim's passionate lunacy, Larry Cadman, was front and center, as always, ready to help bring Jumbo home.

I don't know how we would have gotten Jumbo home if it weren't for these good friends stepping in to help. But I do know they didn't do it just because they are our friends, they did it because Jim's passion compels people to just want to be a part of it all.

We hope sharing our antics helps you to find your passion and avoid catching someone else's lunacy.

THE SCRAMBLER AND THE REINDEER

We were on our way home from a long trip to Alabama to buy two Scrambler cars just like the ones that were on the Scrambler ride at Idora Park. These weren't from Idora but having them in our museum would add the flavor of Idora. When an Idora Park original artifact isn't available we look for something identical. We won't pass something off as Idora Park's if it wasn't at Idora, so we identify it as "Idora Park Identical".

By day three of our return trip conversation between Nuck and me had waned. So, he spent much of the time listening to music through his earbuds. He has a favorite band, The Indigenous Clowns. I've never heard of them except from Nuck. He told me once that they have a few good songs out, "Hey Kid, Pull My Finger!" was one of his favorites. I remember one other title he mentioned, a song called, "Gypsies, Tramps and IRS Agents".

Lately he's been listening to a new girl band that goes by the name of Flat Bottom Gurls. I thought I misheard him, so I asked if he was talking about the song "Fat Bottom Girls" by the band Queen. It was a huge hit song, and I knew that Nuck likes the song. I also suspect that he has a fascination with shapely female behinds. Nuck said no, that the band really is named FLAT BOTTOM GURLS, a female pop band from Korea. Then it made sense to me. Their song, "Do These Pants Look Loose On Me?" was climbing the pop charts. I had no interest in hearing it.

As we made our way north, we had some light snow fall. It was a reminder to us both that Christmas was coming. I had no idea what gift to buy a ninja for Christmas.

Nuck took out his earbuds and turned the radio on to listen to Christmas music. I drove while he sang along to every song, murdering some of the lyrics with his off-key voice. After I heard the third or fourth version of "Rudolph the Red Nosed Reindeer" I had an idea. I was bored, so…

ME: You know that story about Rudolph the Red Nosed Reindeer isn't entirely true. Have you heard the story about what happened to him at Donder Pass?

NUCK: (turning off the radio) Donder Pass? No, Donner Pass, yes. 1800s. Wagon train. California, people freeze, die. People eat people! Yuck! How that relate to Rudolph?

ME: No, not Donner Pass in California, Donder Pass in Pennsylvania. It's almost as gruesome. The other reindeer didn't "love" Rudolph after he led Santa's sleigh on that first foggy Christmas Eve like the song says. They were angry and jealous of Rudolph.

NUCK: Why they angry and jealous? Rudolph save Christmas, every reindeer happy! All little kid happy!

ME: They despised him because he was Santa's "boy", the golden child, the favorite, the head honcho reindeer, numero uno, big man on campus and so on. Also, because Rudolph had a big problem.

NUCK: (puzzled) What problem?

ME: Well, Rudolph liked brussels sprouts, a lot! It was his favorite food. He ate them all the time and it made him flatulent.

NUCK: What flatulent mean?

ME: Well, he was gassy.

NUCK: What gassy mean?

ME: You know, he uh, passed gas - a lot.

NUCK: (confused) Pass gas?

ME: Yes, you know, he uh, vented a vapor trail.

NUCK: (confused) Vent vapor trail?

ME: (rolling my eyes) Do I have to spell it out for you? He caused a stink that the other reindeer had to deal with! He passed gas, he vented vapor, polluted the atmosphere, cut the cheese, ripped loose…

NUCK: (interrupting) Oh! He fart!

ME: Yeah, but I don't like that word. Let's just say he vented gas and being the lead reindeer, the other reindeer were downwind, behind him and didn't appreciate having to smell his emissions.

NUCK: So, Rudolph fart on other reindeer!

ME: Well yeah, but let's not use that particular word. But you know in the song where it goes, "they used to laugh and call him names"? Well, the name they called him was "Fart-a-holic"! That's not nice at all.

NUCK: Yikes! Fart-a-holic! Boss, Rudolph fart! No big deal! Everyone fart sometime.

ME: (changing the subject) Okay look, I just don't like the word. Now, can I tell you the story or shall we turn the radio back on?

NUCK: Tell story, boss. No more fart talk.

ME: Thank you. Now, Santa didn't just use Rudolph for only that one stormy night. Rudolph was the go-to reindeer for every

NUCKED!

Christmas Eve. The other reindeer didn't like that for two reasons. One, Rudolph was younger than all the other reindeer and he sort of assumed the "Lead Reindeer" job over the more senior reindeer. And two, …

NUCK: (cutting me off) He fart on other reindeer.

ME: You said you'd let me tell the story.

NUCK: But I right? 'cause he fart on other reindeer?

ME: (frustrated) Okay, yes, because he farts! Are you happy? I said it. He farts! Now, can I tell the darn story?

NUCK: Tell story, boss.

ME: There were eight other reindeer behind Rudolph. Some of the names vary a bit, depending on who's telling the story. But the way I heard it, their names, besides Rudolph were Dasher, Dancer, Prancer, Vixen, Comet, Cupid, Donder and Blitzen. Donder was also called "Donner". They were all fast reindeer, but the fastest ones were Comet and Blitzen. In fact, Blitzen was so fast that in World War II the German army borrowed his name for their fast method of attack, the blitzkrieg. The word "blitz" in football also comes from Blitzen's name.

NUCK: Really?

ME: No, I just made that up. But it sounds plausible. Anyway, Dasher was the handsomest reindeer. He was "dashing", hence the name Dasher. He's actually the one that all the reindeer loved, not Rudolph like the song says. Dancer, Prancer and Vixen were the females. Dancer and Prancer were the reindeer equivalent of dancing show girls. They performed on reindeer follies or something like that before Santa discovered them. Vixen, well, she had a sordid past. She had been an exotic reindeer dancer in a little club called "HOOFERS" in downtown Elfville. She was the headliner there because of her dance moves and she also had a bigger rack than the other reindeer.

NUCK: What rack mean?

ME: Antlers. That's what they're called, a "rack" of antlers. Her rack was bigger than the other exotic dancers in Elfville. A big rack is attractive to reindeer, I guess. She loved to tease the male reindeer by dressing in these skimpy little collars with tassels on them and she painted her hooves in bright red polish. She also had a larger than average tail that she kept neatly trimmed and she wiggled it a lot. She drove the male reindeer crazy. She left the club scene because she was being stalked by a big bull walrus. Mrs. Clause, Santa's wife heard about Vixen and convinced Santa to take her in. Santa sent a few tough guy elves to talk to the walrus. I guess they made him an offer he couldn't refuse because he never bothered Vixen again. Now about Cupid, he was the peacemaker. He didn't like drama or conflict. He was just a very nice, gentle soul. Rumor has it that he once had an important acting career in a Nativity scene.

But Donder, Donder was conniving. He was always complaining about something or other and trying to get the other reindeer involved in some "reindeer game" or other. He had gambling debts and liked to drink pinecone wine a little too often, if you know what I mean. He was Santa's problem child, but also one of Santa's favorites.

NUCK: What happen to Rudolph?

ME: It was another foggy, snowy night with low visibility and again, Rudolph was leading the other eight reindeer. Santa was way at the back, sitting in his sleigh with that big red magical bag that held all the toys for good girls and boys around the world. Santa was clueless as to Rudolph's gas venting problem. The odor never bothered him because it was well dissipated long before it could reach him. He was too busy to notice anyway because all he did was shout out, "Merry Christmas!" and "Ho, ho, ho!" He even stopped saying, "Now Dasher, now Dancer, now Prancer and Vixen, on Comet, on Cupid, on Donder and Blitzen!" And that bothered the reindeer too because they liked hearing Santa call out their names.

NUCKED!

NUCK: (eyes wide, listening intently) Santa never say Rudolph name!

ME: You're right! Calling Rudolph's name with the other reindeer names didn't sound right. Santa had elves working on a new "chant", but it just wouldn't "flow" smoothly. The closest they could get was, "Now Dasher, now Dancer, now Prancer and Vixen, on Comet, on Cupid, on Donder, on Blitzen! Oh, and you too Rudolph!" It just didn't sound right. So, instead of leaving out Rudolph's name he just stopped calling out all the names. I dunno, a mistake on Santa's part? Maybe! It really upset the other reindeer, even Cupid, but especially Donder.

NUCK: (listening intently) Donder not nice!

ME: (trying not to laugh) Nope, not nice at all. Pretty mean, actually!

NUCK: What happen next?

ME: Santa was sitting in his sleigh, steering the reindeer over Pennsylvania and it was snowing pretty hard. Visibility was low, so Santa increased altitude to get above the snow clouds. When he did this the reindeer had to exert more strength to climb. The stress from added pressure on their bodies from the altitude climb caused Rudolph to let go with a blast of air from his behind.

Rudolph looked over his shoulder and said, "Sorry! Excuse me!" The other reindeer were fed up. They started to grumble amongst themselves, and they weren't paying attention when a big jetliner whooshed by and almost hit them. The tailwind from the jet forced Santa's sleigh to crash land into a snowbank, damaging the runners on Santa's sleigh. No one was hurt, but the other reindeer blamed Rudolph for the crash.

NUCK: (eager and interrupting) 'Cause he fart on other reindeer!

ME: Yeah, kinda. But mainly because he was the lead reindeer and it's his job to guide everyone and keep them safe. Of course, the other reindeer would never take responsibility for losing their focus and grumbling.

NUCK: But Rudolph fart on them! He eat brussel sprout!

ME: Yes, but the other reindeer should still be paying attention to where they're going, no matter what! And please, enough of the fart talk, okay?

NUCK: What happen next? Abonible snowman attack, like in movie?

ME: What? Abonible snowman? What are you talking about? What movie? Do you mean abominable snowman? Because I don't know what "Abonible" means.

NUCK: Yes, Abonible snowman! In Rudolph movie he attack!

ME: Oh, okay. It's starting to make sense now. There was a Rudolph cartoon movie when I was a kid. There was an abominable snowman in the cartoon. And the word is "a-bom-in-a-ble", not whatever it is you said.

NUCK: (excited, nodding) I see movie too. Donder Pass story have Abonible snowman?

ME: (shaking my head) Look, I give up. But no, there's no Abonible snowman at the Donder Pass. Not an abominable one either, just eight tiny reindeer, nine including Rudolph. Oh, and Santa Clause of course. Anyway, Santa was calm during and after the close call with the jet. He can do that thing where he touches his finger to his nose so he can transport himself and the magic bag of toys to wherever he wants to go.

He's able to leave. But he can't do that for the reindeer or the sleigh. So, he told the reindeer to wait there, and he'd send some elves to fix the sleigh, then he'd come retrieve the reindeer and sleigh as soon as Christmas was over. Santa's plan was to shoot back to the North Pole, use his second-string reindeer and sleigh to finish the toy delivery job, then return to Donder Pass for the reindeer and sleigh.

The reindeer didn't like the idea of staying there in the snow and missing Christmas, but they kept their thoughts to themselves. With his finger to his nose, Santa and the magic bag of toys disappeared.

As soon as Santa was gone the arguing started and the tempers flared, and everyone blamed Rudolph. An hour later a plot was hatched.

NUCK: (listening intently) Plot? What they do?

ME: Well, Donder was the ringleader and Blitzen was his best friend, so Blitzen went along with whatever Donder wanted to do. First, they distracted Cupid by asking him to gather firewood so they could keep warm. Rudolph was oblivious to what was going on. He was busy listening to music on his ear buds, kicked back against a big rock, jamming to his tunes. Dasher, the handsome one, was busy too. He was quite vain, always had a mirror on him so he spent much of his time alone, admiring his reflection. Comet liked to keep in shape. He was out running timed sprints while Santa was away. Two of the girls, Dancer and Prancer were practicing show girl dance moves together. That left Vixen, the former exotic dancer from HOOFERS.

NUCK: (excited, interrupting) She have big rack and wiggly tail.

ME: (trying not to laugh) Yes, a big rack and she wiggled her tail. Plus, she wore bright red polish on her hooves and tassels on her collar.

NUCK: (nodding intently) Make boy reindeer crazy!

ME: Yes. Anyway, Donder, Blitzen and Vixen crept away to a secluded cave, well away from the other reindeer. That's where they made their plan, inside that cave. Vixen's job was to go back outside and sit next to Rudolph, strike up a conversation with him, then walk away, wiggling her tail, stop and look over her shoulder at Rudolph who undoubtedly would be watching her closely, then she was to ask him to join her in exploring the cave. Once she had him inside the cave Donder and Blitzen would jump out and deal with Rudolph, once and for all!

NUCK: (worried) They hurt Rudolph?

ME: Let me finish. So, Rudolph dropped his ear buds and followed Vixen as she wiggled her way to the cave. As soon as the two of them were inside the cave, Blitzen jumped out of his hiding spot and blocked the cave entrance. Donder stepped from the shadows. He had an evil smile on his face. Rudolph turned to leave but saw Blitzen standing there. Rudolph knew right away that he was in big trouble. Rudolph turned to look at Vixen, hoping she could explain, but he saw Donder standing next to her now, one front leg around Vixen's shoulder, an evil grin across his mouth. Rudolph was certain now; he was in danger. He looked at Vixen and asked her, "Et tu Vixen?"

NUCK: (alarmed) No! Like Julius Caesar! They stab Rudolph? Kill him?

ME: Donder stepped forward, stood face to face with the frightened, quivering Rudolph. Rudolph thought about running, but Blitzen was blocking the only way out. Rudolph was trapped! Donder reached into the pack he kept on his back, felt around, an evil, knowing grin on his face. When his hoof found the object he was reaching for Donder said, "This is it! This is it for you Rudolph, we've had enough!"

Donder quickly withdrew the object from the pack and shoved it towards Rudolph's chest. Rudolph recoiled in horror, but not quickly enough. He closed his eyes, expecting to feel the dreaded blow find its mark in his chest.

But the blow never came. Rudolph slowly opened one eye and looked at Donder's face, then down at the outstretched hoof. Rudolph was puzzled. What was this? Cradled in Donder's hoof was a small plastic bottle! Rudolph asked, "No knife? I thought you were going to kill me! You aren't going to kill me?"

Donder was surprised by Rudolph's words, "What? Kill you? No, of course not! What? Are you, crazy? This is for you. We're sick of you farting on us all the time. It's called No Mo' Gas. It'll help! Just one swig before we fly and no more farting! And do us a favor, lay off the brussels sprouts on Christmas Eve, will ya?"

NUCKED!

And that's the story of Donder Pass. After that night Rudolph the Red Nosed Reindeer avoided brussels sprouts on work nights and all of the other reindeer loved him.

NUCK: (relieved) I'm glad no one eat Rudolph.

ME: Yep, me too. But I hear that venison can be delicious if prepared right. Next year I'll tell you what happened to Vixen!

SPIKE'S SIDE OF THE STORY

Jim starts this story by telling us he was on his way home from Alabama after getting two scrambler cars. What he didn't tell you was this was our second consecutive weekend on the road to get Idora Park artifacts and we were still living in Northern Virginia.

The weekend before this trip we had driven about 2,500 miles to Florida and back in fewer than four days. We got the Skydiver car on that trip.

No sooner did arrive home that Jim hears of two Scrambler Cars for sale in Southern Alabama. In the truck and on the road to Alabama we go… Another 2,000-mile plus trip in fewer than four days.

Running out of things to talk about and being too tired and giddy to even try was a real thing for us.

And when it gets quiet like that, his mind starts to wander…

Quite frequently he'll break the silence with "I was just thinking about a story…" and then he'll give me the skeleton version of whatever nonsense is rattling around in his brain.

How he came up with Reindeer as the main characters, I'll never know but it was probably tied to discussions about what we would be doing for Christmas that year.

Without a doubt that discussion included grandchildren, whom he often refers to as "Fart-a-holics", even though he really does hate that word…

And the whole exotic dance club thing… well, he's a guy… which means he notices every one of those pretty darn explicit exotic dancer billboard signs that line the highways along the "bible-belt" of America.

As for the fart theme, I have a feeling it's his way of passive aggressively telling me he wished I didn't like brussels sprouts so much. Hmmmmm.

And by the way, fart in Scandinavia means speed or motion… And a fartsdumper? Well, a speed bump of course… Don't say you didn't learn something reading this book.

LIFE LESSON: Take the mint when it's offered

… Or, No Mo Gas. When someone offers you a mint, a piece of gum or some other bodily odor improving solution, it can only mean one of two things.

First, they are just a nice person who was taught to share. In which case, it's only polite to accept their offer and give them the positive reinforcement.

Second, they are passively hoping that whatever the offensive odor is that is emanating from your body will cease and they are willing to do just about anything, including giving up their favorite mint or expensive antacid or anti-flatulent to make it go away.

An addendum to this LIFE LESSON: Always assume it's the former and not the latter situation. By doing so you create a win-win for everyone. Someone gets perceived as nice (even if they were being self-serving) and you get bodily odor improvement.

DEAD THINGS ON A TRAIN

Idora Park had a kiddie train located appropriately enough, in Kiddieland. That train carried an operator and up to 14 kids around an oval track. It was powered by a gasoline engine and rolled  along on a 12-inch-wide track. The Miniature Train Company (MTC) built train #419 and it arrived at Idora Park in 1951 when Kiddieland was constructed on the site once occupied by the swimming pool.

MTC #419 was sold at the Idora Park auction in October 1984. Then, it just disappeared. Rumor had it that the train was somewhere in Alabama.

NUCKED!

We, Nuck and I needed to find out what happened to MTC #419, but never could. Years went by, turning into decades.

But then, …

NUCK: (excited) Boss, you not believe this! I find kiddie train!

ME: Okay, another wild goose chase? Where is it this time? Alabama again?

NUCK: Yes, Ucheekuchee, rhyme with Liberace, kinda. Small town near other small town, Ol, Alabama.

ME: (skeptical) What? Ucheekuchee? What a ridiculous name. You're kidding, right? Near another town named Ol? Who makes up names like that?

NUCK: Honest Boss, I check! Top left part of Alabama! Population 17. Ucheekuchee, rhyme with Liberace, kinda. He famous composer.

I decided that Nuck had had the wool pulled over his eyes by someone trying to rip us off. But when he pulled out an old map and showed me the little town right where he said it was my skepticism began to ease a bit.

As we looked over the map Nuck told me the story. A composer had bought the kiddie train for his property in yes, a very small town called Ucheekuchee, rhymes with Liberace, kinda, in Alabama. The owner was ready to sell the train because he found a larger train for a business he ran as a sideline. Maybe he wasn't too successful at composing music, and he branched out? Seems he had some dealings in petroleum production and needed a bigger train for transporting materials, maybe? I guessed it would all make sense when we got to Ucheekuchee, rhymes with Liberace, kinda.

I made a phone call to the train owner; Alfred VanDeVenter. Everything seemed to check out. A deal was struck for the train providing it was in very good shape. Directions were given and Nuck and I packed for our trip. We attached our car trailer to the truck, synchronized our watches and set off for Ucheekuchee, rhymes with Liberace, kinda.

It was mid-September and weather was cooling in northeast Ohio. I was looking forward to warmer weather down south.

The drive was mostly uneventful, but we noticed more and more roadkill the farther south we went. Dead animals were almost as common as Dollar General stores and ambulance-chasing-attorney billboards. The dead things we saw were mostly raccoons, rabbits, groundhogs, squirrels, the obligatory opossum, a few skunks, deer, coyotes and a few foxes, struck down while crossing the highway. We never saw an alligator, dead or alive.

On day two of our southbound travel, we left Tennessee and entered Alabama. The dead stuff on the road was much the same as' we'd seen in the other states we'd passed through until Nuck pointed out something unusual.

NUCK: (excited and pointing) Boss, look! Giant stink bug!

ME: What? Where?

NUCK: (still excited, pointing out the windshield) Giant stink bug! Dead! Wow! It huge!

I looked in the direction he was pointing and sure enough, there was something ugly lying dead on the side of the road. But, having gotten just a passing glance it didn't look like any stink bug I'd ever seen. What I did see looked odd. I slowed the truck and pulled over onto the shoulder, then noticed a dirt road off to my right. I pulled onto the dirt road, making sure the truck and trailer were not sticking out into traffic. I wanted to see this "giant stink bug", or whatever it was. We jumped out of the truck... and the odor hit us!

ME: (squinting and gagging from the stink) What the...? I've never smelled anything this bad! That stink is disgusting! Maybe it is a giant stink bug or a herd of dead skunks. I think I'm going to throw up!

NUCK: (excited) I tell you Boss! Like I say, big stink bug!

I held my nose and walked closer to the dead thing. Its body was bloated from death and the sweltering heat of an Alabama summer. All four of its legs were sticking up toward the sky with its little tail pointing like an arrow. The head looked undamaged, but there was dried blood under the body. Poor thing!

ME: That's no giant stink bug! That's an armadillo!

NUCK: Arma what? Look like baby tank. That real animal? Maybe toy? Maybe military weapon?

ME: (pointing out the blood) It's real. You'll see armadillos in the south, but not up north. But that stink isn't coming from just this one dead animal. That stink is everywhere around us!

Nuck picked up a stick and bent down to look closer at the dead armadillo. He gently poked one of the critter's legs with the stick.

NUCK: He look like little tank. Like Iron Man suit. He bite, Boss?

ME: Iron Man, eh? That's definitely not an Iron Man suit. And no, the dead ones don't bite. Not many dead animals bite. Too busy being dead. Look, we should be close to Ucheekuchee, rhymes with Liberace, kinda. Let's head back to the truck and check the GPS.

Nuck was still bent down, examining the little armored critter.

NUCK: Boss, all his leg stick up, look like he walk on air.

ME: Or, lying dead on its back which is much more accurate. Come on, let's check the GPS.

As we started back for the truck, I heard a scraping sound behind us. I turned to look. The armadillo was gone. The blood was still there on the ground, but no animal. I looked at Nuck.

ME: (puzzled) That's just a little creepy! What happened to the armadillo? It's gone! Did it just get dragged away by a predator?

NUCK: (shrugging his shoulders) Maybe he not dead. Maybe armadillo play 'possum?

ME: That thing was dead. Dead things don't just up and undead themselves. But where did it go and how did it go?

We heard an engine start in the woods, the sound of it coming from where we'd stood near the armadillo. We took off running toward the sound and found railroad tracks a few feet from the road. Small railroad tracks, like kiddie train small tracks. And, sure enough a little train was chugging away from us on those tracks! Could this be the Idora Park kiddie train? We yelled out to the operator, but he kept going. Maybe he was too far away to hear us? I wondered, did he take the dead armadillo, and if so, why?

We started out on foot, following the tracks through the woods. After maybe a hundred yards a chicken came running out of the woods toward us, startled the heck out of me. I was still a little jumpy from the weirdness of the armadillo getting up and leaving. The chicken stopped in front of Nuck as if it had found its long-lost mother.

NUCK: (startled) What kind of bird, Boss?

ME: Are you kidding? It's a chicken. You've never seen a chicken?

NUCK: (in awe of the strange bird) No Boss, only on dinner plate or in bucket at KFC. Why his head move back and forth when he walk? He get dizzy? He funny!

ME: All chickens walk like that. They do that when they eat too. It's called "pecking". Oh, and it's not a "he" it's a "she". Chickens that look like that are female. It's called a "hen".

NUCK: (puzzled) How that possible? How baby chicken are made if all chicken girls?

ME: (frustrated) Okay, well… there are male chickens, but they aren't hens. They are called "cocks". Uh, er, cock-a-doodle-doos. Better yet, call the males "rooster".

The chicken's behavior was entertaining and comical. It kept running up to Nuck and sort of nuzzling his leg when it wasn't pecking for food on the ground. It was completely ignoring me but was very much attached to Nuck. It would rub against Nuck's legs, run off to peck the ground, then run back to Nuck.

NUCK: Chicken funny how he peck ground. Peck, peck, peck. I like him. He like me. I keep him.

ME: "She", not "he" and you're not keeping it.

NUCKED!

NUCK: (smiling at the chicken) Yes, I keep him. His head move funny. I name him, "Pecker Head".

ME: (shocked) What? NO! You can't name it Pecker Head! And you can't keep it either. And stop calling it "him" it's a female!

Nuck ignored me and couldn't take his eyes off this chicken that was just as obviously smitten with him.

ME: (trying to reason with him) Nuck, look, she probably has a family. You don't want to take her away from her family. There might be a cock, er, I mean a mister chicken and little baby chicks at home waiting for their mama!

NUCK: Okay Boss. Maybe he just hang out for a while. If he not go home I keep Pecker Head.

ME: Look, you really can't keep calling that thing Pecker Head. It's not a nice name. And it's accustomed to living out here in the wild. It wouldn't make a good pet. And again, it's not a "he" it's a "she".

NUCK: (ignoring me) Come, Pecker Head! We find kiddie train now.

I cringed at the name.

ME: Nuck seriously, give the chicken another name. And I'll be okay with that. Pick anything. I don't care, but Pecker Head has to go.

NUCK: Any name?

ME: Any name!

NUCK: I call him "Pecker", no "Head"!

ME: Ummm, no! It's the same name.

NUCK: Boss, you say ANY name! I pick Pecker!

ME: (frustrated) Fine! Call the darn thing Pecker. I'm tired of arguing about it. You and that chicken have been a big distraction. Now, let's go find that train!

We walked on, following the tracks, hopefully in the direction that leads us to the train. Nuck kept right on talking to the chicken like it was his best friend and the chicken stuck right with him. So did the odor in the air. Neither the chicken nor the stench in the air was leaving. In fact, the stink seemed to be getting stronger the longer we walked. It smelled like a mixture of dead animals, old gasoline and fresh asphalt. Disgusting!

We finally came to a clearing with three huge concrete silos in a row. The silos had to be about 30 feet tall and maybe 20 feet around. A farm? It sure did stink though. The horrible odors seemed to be coming from the silos, but I wasn't sure. The stench was everywhere. Each silo had writing on the side. The silo on the left read "Beet Oven" the one in the middle read "Tchai Coffee" and the silo on the right read "Puew Chini". We walked past the stinking silos until we saw an old mobile home just behind the "Beet Oven" silo.

NUCK: Boss, someone live there? How people live in stink smell?

ME: (hushing him) Not so loud! This must be someone's home. There's a crudely hand painted sign in front of the trailer that reads "Nosmo King". Maybe the King's know Alfred VanDeVenter, the music composer who owns the Idora kiddie train. Look, the train tracks run right through here!

We heard a door open to the mobile home. A stooped, white-bearded man stepped out and waved, asked how he might be of service.

ME: You must be Mr. King? We're sorry to intrude, but we followed these tracks hoping to find the owner of the train. His name is Alfred VanDeVenter, a music composer who lives in Ucheekuchee. Is this Ucheekuchee by any chance? Do you know Mr. VanDeVenter?

ALFRED: Heh, heh! Yep! Yer in Ucheekuchee, rhymes with Liberace, kinda and yep, yer lookin' at him. I'm Alfred VanDeVenter, but you can call me Al. And I ain't no music composer. Where'd you get that notion? I do like music, but heck I ain't no composer. I can't even play an instrument. I can play the jukebox when I got a dime and that's about it. Heh, heh! Why'd you call me Mr. King?

NUCKED!

ME: (pointing) Well, that sign over there says "Nosmo King", so I just figured…

ALFRED: (chuckling) Heh, heh! That sign don't say "Nosmo King". That sign says, "No Smoking". Cain't have no flames near here with all that gas vapor in the air. We'd all get blowed up! Heh, heh.

ME: (rolling my eyes) My partner here said you were a composer. I never brought it up when we talked on the phone. I just assumed…

ALFRED: (cutting me off) Heh, heh. Funny how rumors get started. No, not a composer. I'm a comPOSTER. I COMPOST. Sounds a bit like composer I s'pose. I take roadkill and compost them in those three big silos behind you. I'm makin' my own oil and gasoline! Fossil fuel… kinda. Heh, heh.

I turned to look at the three huge silos and saw that they were lettered the same on this side as the other side, the side we saw when we had first arrived. "Beet Oven", "Tchai Coffee" and "Puew Chini".

Well, we just discovered exactly what causes the big stink.

ME: So, you aren't making beets or coffee or whatever Puew Chini is? You're making gasoline?

ALFRED: (pointing at the silos) Heh, heh! Yessiree! My own oil and gas. I named the compost silos after famous musicians. Maybe that's how folks think I'm a composer? That one's Beethoven, that one rightcher is Tchaikovsky and yonder is Puccini. Beethoven takes yer larger roadkill, like coyotes, deer, sometimes a cow or a horse. Tchaikovsky gets the sweeter, smaller critters like squirrels, raccoons, groundhogs, armadillos, even snakes. Puccini ain't as picky. He takes the smellier stuff; skunks, 'possum, rats, mice, the occasional pig, even has a taste for buzzards. Puccini stinks up the place, but he's my money maker. Someday we're gonna be pumpin' high octane fuel outta Puccini, yessir! That little Idory train has been a real workhorse for me, haulin' them dead varmints to the silos all these years. Heh, heh!

Just as I had suspected, the train was transport for Alfred's roadkill fuel project. Yuck! My head was swimming, partly from the stench, but also the crazy notion that old Alfred here thinks he's going to be making his own fuel from roadkill animals. I resisted the urge to mention his spelling of "Beethoven", "Tchaikovsky" and "Puccini". Today wasn't the day for a spelling lesson.

Meanwhile, Nuck was too busy playing with his chicken to pay attention to the conversation.

ME: How long have you been composting like this and how much oil and gas have you gotten so far?

ALFRED: (rubbing his chin and looking skyward) Heh, heh! Well, you know it takes a while. Every month or so we're squeezing out a few drops of some concoction that we burn in the oil lamps. But we're in it for the long haul. Heh, heh!

I couldn't help but wonder if it might be smarter to somehow tap the horrible gasses emanating from the silos. At least it's burnable methane, I think. Then again, maybe a spark would cause the whole contraption to explode. Nuck and I needed to get out of there fast.

ME: (in an effort to see the train) Well hey, why don't we look at that Idora Park kiddie train and if it's truly MTC #419 and in the condition you said over the phone, we can complete the deal, load it and the railroad track onto my trailer and be on our way?

ALFRED: Heh, heh! Why sure, but I wouldn't be a good southern gentleman if I didn't offer you two some good old southern cooking. Oh, and you brought foldin' money, right? I don't take newfangled payment like checks or money orders, just foldin' money. Heh, heh.

Checks and money orders are "newfangled"?

ME: (stifling a smirk) Nope, no, nothing newfangled. I'm strictly oldfangled.

Alfred nodded, smiled at me, turned toward his trailer, and yelled out, "Heh, heh! Martha Rae let's get these Yankees fed a good meal 'afore we complete business. I seen a delicious looking yardbird out here that fits the bill! Grab that meat cleaver Martha Rae! Heh, heh!'".

There's no way I would be capable of eating with that stench surrounding us. Just breathing that stink was about all I could do, and just barely. I had no appetite and just wanted to get the train and leave. I needed a distraction and an exit plan.

I was curious though. Alfred said "yardbird". What's a yardbird? Some southern bird? I didn't see any birds on the premises except for Nuck's chicken. But that's a chicken, not a yardbird.

Alfred pointed the way toward his trailer home. Nuck and I reluctantly followed. Martha Rae passed us on her way outside and nodded a toothless grin. She had a meat cleaver in her hand.

Alfred, Nuck and I sat at a rectangular table in the kitchen to discuss the kiddie train. Alfred told us he'd bought it long ago from a Circus Fatman in Ohio. The Fatman used the train as part of his circus gig. He'd ride the train around inside the circus tent while blowing up balloons and twisting them into animals for the kids.

Eventually, the Fatman thought he and his act were much more valuable than they were. He constantly complained that he was being ripped off and even demanded that the circus owner place a plaque with the Fatman's name on the circus tent. Instead, the circus owner canned him. Fired, the Fatman had no choice but to sell the kiddie train. Sad story, sad Fatman. Narcissism's greed kills relationships.

Martha Rae came back into the trailer, one hand gripping a chicken by the neck and a meat cleaver in the other hand. The chicken was obviously in distress, flapping its wings like crazy. She laid the chicken on a chopping block right there in the kitchen and raised the meat cleaver high…

The chicken looked familiar. Where's the yardbird?

That's when things got crazy…

NUCK: (jumping from his chair, screaming) MY PECKER! LET GO MY PECKER!

I gulped! He didn't really say that did he?!

MARTHA RAE: (shocked, flustered by the outburst) Excuse me?! What did you say? You watch your language, or I'll put you over my knee and spank your little bottom!

NUCK: (still yelling) YOU CHOKE MY CHICKEN! LET GO MY PECKER! DON'T CHOP MY PECKER! AIEEEEE!

Martha Rae looked stunned. Alfred looked stunned. I was stunned. Nuck was furious!

ME: (trying to calm Nuck) Okay, look, she heard you! She's not going to chop Pecker's head, right ma'am? Besides, she said she was getting yardbird. That's a chicken! Let it go!

MARTHA RAE: (surprised, indignant and still gripping Nuck's Pecker by the neck) What in blue blazes do you think a yardbird is? It's a chicken! They's one and the same thin'. This one was wanderin' around outside so I grabbed her. How was I to know it's his? Who in their right mind has a chicken for a pet, let alone name it Pecker? That's a word that we southern folk do not use for a name!

ME: (pleading) Look, we're really sorry about the name. We're from the unwashed north. We didn't know that name was a no-no. But could you please let go of the poor thing? You're choking Nuck's chicken and if you don't let go, you're going to see a ninja turn into the Tasmanian Devil! You don't want to experience that!

Martha Rae took the cue, dropped the chicken and Nuck's little Pecker took off running through the open doorway.

ALFRED: (chiming in) Heh, heh! Okay, well I guess there's no chicken or yardbird for dinner. We can go into town and celebrate our deal at a fancy restaurant. We got a Burger Barn not 10 miles away. Heh, heh.

ME: Uh, you know, I think Nuck and I have kind of lost our appetite in the excitement. Why don't we close the deal on the kiddie train and you folks go on to dinner without us? We'll just load up the train and the stack of tracks that go with it and be on our way.

Alfred and Martha Rae looked at each other and appeared to agree with my recommendation. Finally, Alfred looked at me, stuck out his hand for the payment we'd earlier agreed on and I counted out the foldin' money. The deal was done. Or so I thought.

ALFRED: (pointing) The train and rest of them tracks are in the barn. You can use the hose in the barn to clean the blood and guts off the train once you get the roadkill out of the seats. I'd much appreciate it if you'd put the armadillos in the Tchaikovsky silo. The skunks, opossum and rats go in Puccini. Heh, heh.

NUCK: (shocked and disgusted) Blood? Guts? Roadkill? Boss, you clean train. I find my Pecker.

And that, folks, is how we acquired the Idora Park kiddie train. As for Nuck's Pecker? I think the trauma of being choked and nearly beheaded was too much for her. We last saw her squawking loudly as she ran out of the VanDeVenter's trailer, heading for the woods, her love affair with Nuck seemingly ended. Nuck searched high and low for him. I mean "her", but with no success.

By the time a dejected Nuck returned from the fruitless Pecker search I had finished the job he stuck me with, hosing the dead animal goo off the train. We loaded the train cars and tracks onto my trailer and started north, for home in Ohio. Ucheekuchee, which rhymes with Liberace, kinda, was in our rear-view mirror.

Nuck, his little 3'-3" ninja self, tucked into his car seat, strapped to the front passenger seat, was eating a bag of his favorite comfort food, Fritos.

NUCK: (sadly) I miss my Pecker. But I okay Boss. It not meant to be. Hungry though. We go eat?

ME: I'm glad you're taking it so well. Pecker really liked you, but I guess you're right, it just wasn't meant to be. But hey, I'm hungry too and I'm pretty sure I saw a KFC just a few miles back the way we came! Heh, heh.

NUCK: You not funny, Boss!

ME: Gee, I hope you're wrong.

SPIKE'S SIDE OF THE STORY

Our travels have taken us all over this beautiful country of ours and with that has come more than our fair share of roadkill sightings. It's a bit of a contest between us to see who can identify the newest swollen bloody mess on the road the quickest. I almost always lose. Sometimes spectacularly. Once, I argued to no avail that I saw the dead squirrel first. Jim of course won that battle on the grounds that it was actually a very large, belly distended, raccoon, which dead or alive, looks nothing like a squirrel. That's when he unilaterally added the rule that misidentifying a critter is grounds for disqualification. We laugh about it but whenever we have a debate of what a dead critter is, he wins by default.

One time, while traveling through the everglades in Florida, we were both stumped, and very curious, about what a very large dark colored heap of roadkill was. Jim decided we should go back and take a closer look, so he zipped the car around and we passed it going the opposite direction. That didn't help. It was too far away to get a good look. He zipped the car around again and we passed it for the third time, going much slower trying to get a better look. Still no clue. With curiosity getting the better of him, Jim stopped the car about 50 feet beyond the critter, got out of the car and walked back for a closer look.

I watched from the car and was alarmed when, before he even got within 10 feet of the critter, he did an abrupt about face and high-tailed it back to the car. I figured it was a bear and he wasn't taking any chances getting too close.

I was wrong, which doesn't happen very often in our marriage. Except when it comes to the roadkill identification game, and then I am almost always wrong.

Jim saw the claws and fangs on this monstrosity of a creature and decided he wasn't waiting around to find out if this cat was dead or just playing 'possum. He started the car, and we took off down the road.

What was the critter you ask? Well, I'm not so sure critter is a good word to describe it because that seems to insinuate something sweet about the creature. There is nothing sweet about a Jaguar. Unless of course you're talking about the car.

Who knew Florida had Jaguars (other than the car or football player kind)? We sure didn't. But that was the last time either of us got out of a vehicle to inspect roadkill.

Our roadkill sightings through the years might have been the fodder for this almost completely fabricated kiddie train story. Well, some of it is true, we have traveled to some backwoods places and the characters described in this story might be an amalgamation of some of the characters we've met on our adventures.

We've also wondered if in the world of biodiesel creation, could roadkill become a fuel source... I mean wouldn't that be somewhat ironic. Roadkill used as a fuel source for the vehicles that create roadkill. That's the cycle of life... or death, such as it is.

By the way, how do you pronounce diesel? I pronounce it with the S as an S sound. Jim pronounces it with the S as a Z sound. Okay, before you go look it up and send me a bunch of messages about how I am wrong because the English pronunciation is with a Z sound, I'd like to point out that it is a German word. The diesel engine and fuel were named after their inventor, Adolf Diesel. The German pronunciation is with an S sound. So, in its purest sense, I'm right. As always. Well, almost always. Unless of course we are talking roadkill critters. Ah, but I digress.

What's the real scoop on getting the kiddie train? We got it from a local collector who'd had it in storage for many years. It was one of the earliest, largest, and most expensive purchases we've ever made for The Idora Park Experience except for building the building and doing all the work associated with that.

Jim had the idea that we'd set the train up on its track and let kids ride it. The engine worked and we acquired a train crossing sign and some track with it. Should be easy, right? Seriously, by now you all know better. Nothing is ever easy when it comes to this stuff.

The train crossing sign was rusted and didn't work but we were able to restore it and our friend, Larry Cadman, got the bells and lights working.

The track was a different story. There wasn't much that was usable because it had rusted and rotted away from years of sitting outside in the weather. Troubleshooting 101: when what you have won't work, find something that will. Jim went on the hunt and found a cache of G-12 track for sale in New Jersey. Another road trip adventure in the books and we were the new owners of a trailer load of G-12 track. Yippee! Almost there!

The next step… get the museum open and let the kiddos ride the very same Kiddie Train their parents and grandparents did.

But alas, the Canfield Township Zoning Board saw it differently and deemed that no such rides would be taking place. That's kind of a deal breaker. But we often think… what they don't know won't hurt them… Unfortunately, we know that if we did let anyone ride, they'd find out and we'd be in deep doo-doo.

But who knows, maybe someday…

LIFE LESSON: A good pecker is worth the fight

Nuck loved that Pecker. So much so that when it was threatened, he didn't think about it, he jumped into the fight, and didn't stop until he'd won.

In life there are moments when you just can't help yourself, the fight or flight instinct kicks in and you can even surprise yourself with your actions. But there are times when it can be hard to know what to do and when that happens, doing nothing can feel like the safest thing. But rarely is it.

Jim has always been a fighter… me, not so much. I'm usually the one negotiating toward the middle; maybe not a win for everyone but not a loss either, something palatable for all.

But I too have been surprised when my fight instinct kicked into overdrive, and I didn't let go until I'd won… or at least not lost.

The Idora Park Experience has been a wild ride for us, and we've had to be very judicious about choosing when (and how) to fight or walk away. You wouldn't think that trying to save the memories of multiple generations would require that much fight. We certainly didn't. And it shouldn't. Yet here we are.

We've fought to get several of the artifacts from situations where they were rotting away and nearly forgotten and lost forever. We've fought to share this collection with everyone. And we fought, and everyone lost, when we wanted to open more often, have French fries and cotton candy (made with the original recipes and equipment), and have a few interactive experiences like Kiddie Train rides available.

We believe the fights have been worth it. We hope you do too. And hopefully, when the time comes for The Idora Park Experience to go to the next level others will decide it's worth it and step into the ring (or get on the train) with us.

We'll see…

THE BEAST IN THE BUNKER

Before I begin to tell you of this adventure I must say, yes Spike, opossum really does begin with the letter "O"!

A friend of mine lucked into an amazing gig. To make a long story short, this friend, Jack left the military and went to work for a start-up company that designed, built and flew the earliest generation of drones. The company owner's only child, a daughter worked there too. Jack and the daughter went out on a date and things clicked. Fifteen years later the dad has retired and gifted the business to his daughter who in turn made Jack the President and CEO. The company? Mantis Drone.

Never heard of Mantis Drone? I should think not! They do Top Secret drone surveillance work of the highest level. In order to do this kind of work Jack had an extensive background investigation from the Defense Intelligence Agency. Jack's security clearance is one that's so high and so secret that I'd never heard of it. His clearance is Top Secret/Highest Information Technology (TS/HIT). There are only a few people in the entire country with a TS/HIT.

Jack owed me a favor. A big favor. He wouldn't have that clearance if I hadn't saved his behind from a court martial. I had investigated Jack. He'd worked for me in the military and got in trouble when he was caught in a compromising "event" with our base commander's wife of all people! The two of them were caught skinny dipping in the base water tank! I went to bat for Jack, explaining to our unit commander how embarrassing this would be to our base commander's career if the reason for Jack's punishment were somehow up channeled to higher headquarters. I knew the military game. The base commander didn't do anything wrong, but he'd be the butt of many closed-door jokes. His career progression would be stalled. The brass begrudgingly agreed and charges against Jack were dropped. Jack was a free man, but with a debt. He had to reimburse the base for draining and sanitizing the used water tank. He also owed me for saving his career. And I was ready to call in that marker.

Here's what happened…

Rumors circulated that a small hidden bomb shelter was located on the Idora Park property. The shelter was supposedly built in the late 1940s or very early 1950s when the fear of Russian nuclear attack gripped the country. Unfortunately, all records of Idora Park burned in the 1984 fire. No one seemed to know where this bunker was located or if it really existed. People even scoured the Idora Park grounds with metal detectors, but no one ever found a bunker.

Then, an elderly gentleman came to one of our museum openings and pulled me aside to tell me a story that his father had told him. There is a bunker, but it wasn't built in the 1940s or 1950s. In fact, the bunker is even older. It was built as early as 1903 and used by the trolley company that founded Idora Park. They stored some of their equipment there, especially the trolley scrolls that constantly needed changing because Youngstown was growing with new streets and new landmarks. I'll fill you in later about trolley scrolls.

If I could find that bunker, there might be some amazing Idora Park artifacts still stored there. But how does one scour 26 acres of land to find an underground bunker that no one else has ever found? That's when I thought of Jack, his drone company and the favor he owes me. I made a phone call…

ME: Jack, remember me? I saved your neck when you were caught skinny dipping with the base commander's wife in a water tower a few years back.

JACK: (voice shaky) Uh, yes sir. I remember you. Um, that was a long time ago. A big mistake on both my part and hers. Um, can I ask why you're calling? That was a long time ago.

ME: Well, I need a favor and you're just the man for the job…

I filled him in on what I was looking for and we came up with a plan. It involved infra-red sensors, ground penetrating seismic sensors and drones.

Two drones were enlisted to solve the puzzle. Not just any drones. Jack's company designed and built top secret robotic pigeon drones. They look just like real pigeons, but they are drones with the ability to locate underground resources by use of infra-red or seismic sensors mounted on their belly. Anyone who happens to see the drones will think it's just a pigeon. The problem though, is that pigeons have natural predators. A predator could attack the life-like pigeon, thinking it's actual prey.

Jack's company came up with a solution for protecting their pigeon drones, fitting them with a protective "chaff" mechanism. Chaff is a countermeasure of thin strips of metal foil that aircraft use for protection to confuse enemy missiles from downing the aircraft. The chaff is deployed from the rear of a plane when enemy missiles are launched. The pigeon drone has its own special brand of chaff, not metal foil, but a tiny spray canister filled with fox urine to protect the drone from would-be predators.

The canister is deployed automatically by the pigeon's onboard proximity alert warning system (PAWS) when its sensors detect that a predator is nearby. Urine canisters have been in use for years in military drones. Pigeon drones use the "Predator In Sector Spray" defense, best known by the acronym "PISS". Any predator attempting to attack the pigeon is going to vacate the area pronto when they get a whiff of fox PISS out of fear of becoming an item on the fox's menu.

Jack named his pigeon drones Pink and Floyd.

There's no way that the tiny, but powerful CalLithium3pii battery that powers each pigeon drone could maintain enough charge to fly to Ohio from Jack's company in Ferando, Virginia, scan the Idora property, then return to Jack without recharging. That's a lot of wing flapping. So, Jack loaded up his van and drove the pigeons to Youngstown. We met up on a Saturday, in Canfield, Ohio. Close enough to Idora Park to monitor the pigeon drones via their built-in cameras, but far enough away to not draw attention to what we were doing.

The pigeons, Pink and Floyd were in a protective case. Each drone surrounded by form-fitting, soft pliable foam. One drone uses infra-red to scan, the other uses seismic pulses. I couldn't tell them apart.

ME: So, which one's Pink?

JACK: (pointing at the pigeon on the left side of the case) That's Pink, he uses infra-red.

NUCK: (pointing) That other one Floyd?

ME: (rolling my eyes) Of course it's… no, unfortunately, Floyd couldn't make it. He called in sick. That one is Elton John!

JACK: (laughing) Actually, we're working on a pair of pink flamingo drones and we're calling them Elton and John. But yes Nuck, the other pigeon is Floyd. He's the one with seismic sensors.

NUCK: Do you use girl names?

JACK: We have a chickadee drone that we named Dolly Parton, but we're having aerodynamic problems with the airframe. We think it's too top heavy so we're going to shift some weight to the rear and rename it Kim Kardashian. We'll figure it out.

After a preflight checklist was completed, we watched as Pink and Floyd flapped their wings and took off, headed for Idora Park. Jack switched to camera mode, and we were seeing everything from the pigeon's "view". It seemed like we were actually flying high above traffic. Not expecting that, I was immediately hit with vertigo.

Within minutes Pink and Floyd were over Idora Park and conducting grid pattern scans of the land. Data was being uploaded real-time to Jack's computer as we watched the live feed.

Suddenly, we saw movement! An opossum was scurrying in the area of what was once the Arcade building. The thing was moving north, toward the upper midway, but then it stopped and turned east. The funny thing was, it was running on three legs, one front leg, both back legs. It was carrying something under the other front leg. I asked Jack if he could have one of the drones get a closer look at what the opossum had under its "arm".

Pink dove in for a closer look. The opossum never heard him

coming. We saw what looked like a bottle under the opossum's arm. The opossum was heading straight for the last remaining fire hydrant on Idora Park. There were only two fire hydrants on Idora Park. Neither one worked when fire broke out on April 26, 1984. Hence, Idora burned and closed that year. We have the other fire hydrant in our museum. It was located on the Southeast side of the lower midway. The opossum was headed to the older hydrant, the first one, placed on the park back at Idora's beginning. Actually, before Idora's beginning. The thing is dated 1898. Idora opened a year later.

The live feed from Pink's camera was crystal clear. The opossum went right up to the fire hydrant, looked around as if he was checking to see if he was being followed, saw or heard Pink hovering nearby and hissed a warning at the pigeon drone. I thought Pink might take that action as a threat and engage his PISS defense, but he or it did not. The opossum set down the thing he was carrying, and Pink's lens zoomed in. It was a bottle all right. The label read "Cognac". There was just a small trace of golden-brown liquid in the bottle.

Then, the opossum did something really strange. It stood on its hind legs, put its front legs against the hydrant, then pushed. The hydrant slid backward, revealing a large hole. The opossum picked up the Cognac bottle, ran into the hole, then from inside the hole it pushed the hydrant pack into position, covering the hole again.

Holy cow! How could an opossum move that fire hydrant? How did it learn about the hole? What else might be in that hole? Is it possible that the opossum's hole might be the legendary bunker? If so, no wonder no one found it. Who would think to use a metal detector near a metal fire hydrant? Brilliant! Well, maybe. We had some footwork to do. And, what's up with the Cognac?

We were pretty sure that we'd found our hidden bunker. The two pigeon drones didn't find any other hidden cavernous areas under Idora Park's surface. So, Jack had Pink and Floyd return to Canfield where he boxed them up and the three of them headed home to Ferando, Virginia.

Nuck and I started our investigation. We needed to learn about opossums and Cognac. I knew only that opossums are ugly. I knew less about Cognac. What I found out was eye opening.

Opossums have an affinity for Cognac! It seems, that in the opossum world they refer to Cognac simply as Yak, which makes sense because Cognac is kind of difficult to say and spell even for a human. I can't imagine how difficult it might be for an opossum. Cognac is pronounced "Cone-Yak", kind of. So, again, shortening it to Yak makes it easier to say.

We, Nuck and I, decided to assign a name to the opossum and use that name for our very own secret operation. Nuck pitched in…

NUCK: Boss, call 'possum "Steve"!

ME: Operation Steve? Seriously? Forget it. I was thinking something along the lines of Operation Drunk Opossum.

NUCK: Steve good name, Boss.

ME: Steve is a terrible name for any animal. How about Ollie Opossum?

NUCK: Maybe, or Melvin Marsupial?

ME: Well, that's a little better than Steve. But I like Ollie better. Ollie Opossum!

NUCK: Maybe we flip coin, boss? Head I win, Tail you lose.

ME: Very funny Nuck. But, okay, I'll flip for naming rights. You can call it in the air.

I flipped a quarter into the air. Nuck called "Head". He won.

Three days later we were set to begin Operation Melvin.

I needed to buy some Cognac!

Cognac is a specific type of brandy distilled twice from white wine in copper pot stills and aged in oak barrels – in France of all places! Cognac comes from the town for which it's named, Cognac France. Oui! The stuff is aged for a minimum of two years and the distillation season is a five-month period, October 1 through March 31. Why am I telling you all of this? Well, because we need Cognac to lure the creature away from his bunker-lair so we can search the bunker for any Idora Park treasure that might still be in there. Cognac would be our bait!

Operation Melvin Marsupial was set for mid-November.

Phase 1 of Operation Melvin Marsupial: Buy up all the Cognac from the surrounding liquor stores. Melvin wasn't happy when he couldn't get his Yak fix. Nuck followed the little opossum around town and watched him throw temper tantrum after temper tantrum at the Cognac-empty liquor stores. Melvin, unaware of our surveillance, probably suspected that some other opossum had invaded his turf and was buying up all the Yak. But who knows what really goes on in the mind of an opossum? Honestly, I was shocked to learn that unlike most opossums, Melvin seemed capable of crossing the road without getting hit by a car.

In Phase 2 of our operation, Nuck strategically placed a bottle of Hennessey, a popular brand of Cognac near the bunker opening, opened the bottle, ran for concealment, then waited…

Sure enough, minutes later Melvin came out of the bunker, rubbing sleep from his eyes and licking his dry, chapped lips when suddenly, his head jerked back, and his nose went up in the air! His nostrils caught the familiar, sweet scent of Yak!

Nuck watched and waited in silence.

Melvin ran to his prize, attacking that bottle like a starving baboon on a ripe banana. Melvin guzzled and gulped down half the bottle before stopping to quickly look left and right, probably wondering who left the Yak. Then once again, standing on two hind legs Melvin tipped the bottle to his lips and drained it. Melvin was toast, glassy eyed and having a tough time keeping his balance. He dropped the bottle and wobbled toward the bunker, stopping every few inches to catch his balance. He looked like he was going to make it to the bunker. This was not going to plan. We didn't want Melvin in the bunker when Phase 3 was initiated; Extraction: Enter the bunker and seize whatever it was from Idora Park that Melvin was guarding… if anything.

Nuck kept watching, hoping the Yak would render Melvin unconscious. Then, just before Melvin reached the bunker he teetered to his left, then tottered to his right, then dropped to whatever knees are called on an opossum. Melvin's head was swaying like he had bed spins, then BLAM, his body dropped, landing flat on his stomach. In his drunken haze he managed to roll over on his back, his paw reaching for the empty Yak bottle, but passing out in the process. He was out like a light, snoring on the ground near the bunker opening.

Time to enter the secret bunker!

Nuck moved quickly and quietly, sliding past the comatose opossum as he entered the bunker. Once inside he flicked on his night vision goggles so he could see in the darkness and scan the bunker's interior. Then he saw it, propped against a curved wall, the artifact, a scroll! A TROLLEY SCROLL! Nuck gently and carefully lifted the delicate artifact and made his exit, tiptoeing silently past the snoring Melvin, empty bottle of Yak by his side. Operation Melvin Marsupial Complete and Successful!

Nuck headed for home.

This trolley scroll possibly dates to Idora Park's earliest days, maybe as far back as 1899 when Idora first opened, as Terminal Park.

Electric trolleys transported people to Idora Park in those early years. There were no cars or buses to do so until a decade or so later. Each trolley scroll had several destinations printed on them. The trolley operator would manually rotate the scroll so riders would know which trolley to ride. Nowadays, buses, subways and trains generally use LEDs fed by GPS instead of scrolls.

As for Melvin, hopefully when he awoke, he wasn't too upset about the missing scroll. We left him an extra bottle of Yak to help ease his pain, just in case.

SPIKE'S SIDE OF THE STORY

For the record, the only marsupial found in North America is the Didelphis Virginiana (Virginia Opossum/Possum). And according to *Merriam-Webster,* "Both **possum** and **opossum** correctly refer to the Virginia opossum frequently seen in North America. In common use, *possum* is the usual term; in technical or scientific contexts *opossum* is preferred. *Opossum* can be pronounced with its first syllable either voiced or silent." I'll just leave it at that and let everyone decide for themself how they want to spell and pronounce it. We finally settled the discussion in our house... we call all possums, "Melvin".

I'm always surprised when Jim weaves some far-fetched tale on Facebook and people go right along with him, never delineating fact from fiction. Sometimes it seems the more far-fetched it is, the more apt people are to believe it.

As evidence, I present just a few of the questions we received after Jim posted the original but modified and condensed "Melvin" story on Facebook: "Opossum drink Cognac?", "Which bunker in Idora Park?", and "How did you learn that the scroll was in there?".

My personal favorite came when an individual who shall remain nameless (to protect us both) was visiting the museum. He was scanning the expanse of the building in awe when he suddenly zoned-in on the trolley scroll mounted on the wall.

I could almost hear the gasp as he realized the treasure before him was the legendary scroll. He leaned very slowly sideways toward me, hinting of a secret he was about to indiscreetly share, and said very quietly, "I can't believe you found that in an underground bunker in Idora Park."

That's good... because we didn't.

Pssst... Jim made it up! Yes! Really!

I know you find that hard to believe... but yes, it's fiction. He does it all the time!

Besides, opossum don't even like Cognac. They stick strictly with rum & coke... go ahead, ask one. Do it before he crosses the road though because they don't usually make it back across...

Seriously, how interesting would it be if he told you the dull, dry truth... we bought the scroll on eBay!

eBay! Yep! Pretty boring, eh? It would be a one sentence story that no one would read, much less care about.

And they certainly wouldn't come visit the museum or buy this book.... You did buy this book, right?

Well, I hope you bought it... our retirement funds are blowing in the wind and Jim tells me he has a line on another "Holy Grail from Idora", UGH...! I thought we were done with this gig!

The point of it all... Idora Park was about fun... frivolity and laughter... And with each passing day, the memories and stories from Idora Park get sweeter... and yes, better tasting, for those who experienced them.

Don't believe me? Ask anyone who ever went to Idora Park to tell you about the French fries...

You can watch them drool as their thoughts wander back in time and they recount how much they loved those hot greasy fries, and how they heard that they were cooked in old dirty lard (yep, they never changed it)… and how the white paper cone shaped cup they were served in fit perfectly in your hand… and how they'd cover the fries in salt and then drench them in malt vinegar until they were more liquid than solid.

And when they tell you how they've never had anything like it since… you believe them. I bet you can taste those fries right now, can't you?

See… it all just gets better with time… and telling of course.

It just wouldn't do Idora Park justice if our stories didn't evoke those same feelings of fun, frivolity and laughter.

Just because there's a bit of fiction sprinkled in with the story doesn't make the adventure itself, or its outcome, any less important or exciting.

Jim and I get to experience the adventures personally, along with all their ups and downs… and his stories are our way of sharing that emotional ride.

So, nope, The Idora Park Experience will never be a "just the facts" story… Because Idora Park and the people who loved her, deserve better.

Jim considers his stories to be "stone soup"… start out with a boring old story, add a sprinkle of truth here, a little dash of experience there, 1/2 cup of BS, a touch of hilarity, stir briskly, bring it to a boil… and presto-change-o… you have a story about some amazing artifact and our adventure bringing it home to the museum for all to enjoy!

LIFE LESSON: Don't just live it, share it

When things get crazy, we joke that it wouldn't be us if it wasn't an adventure.

We've gotten so used to it that we just go into everything expecting it, embracing it, and using our past adventures as coping mechanisms for whatever comes our way.

And when everything is going wrong, or we can't figure out how to make something work, we laugh and say… "Remember when…?", recounting some other adventure that went terribly wrong and ended up amazing… And it's quickly followed with "Well, it's going to make a great story…".

Inevitably we find the fortitude to keep going and figure out the humorous story in it that we can share with all of you.

This whole thing would have been so boring and quite frankly, I think we would have quit a long time ago, if we hadn't been able to figure out how to share it with all of you and bring you along on this wild ride.

NUCKED!

We consider ourselves blessed to have experienced so many adventures in creating The Idora Park Experience. We never set out to do so, but it just seems to have worked out that way.

Occasionally, though, like with the Trolley Scroll, there is no adventure, just a simple payment via PayPal to a mysterious seller hidden behind a veil of anonymity on the internet, and voila the artifact shows up on our doorstep a few days later.

What's my point you ask? Go live your adventures…! Exhale when they are crazy, appreciate when they are not and remember to share your stories… and maybe stretch the truth just a bit… in a fun way, of course… so others can live the adventure too.

THE MOUNTAIN LION AND THE WILDCAT

Our Idora Park collection continued to grow, but something was missing, and it nagged at me. I wanted to obtain five Wildcat Rollercoaster cars. Five Rollercoaster cars would complete a Wildcat train. Idora's Wildcat had three trains; each train was painted a different color and consisted of five cars per train.

There was a yellow train, a blue train and an orange train. We owned four cars of different colors: one yellow, one blue and two orange. One of those orange cars had been beautifully restored and repainted yellow. It didn't matter to me that the four cars were not all the same color or from the same train, but I wanted a fifth car; to complete a five-car train. Having five cars would also mean that we had one-third of Idora Park's Wildcat Rollercoaster cars.

Of the 15 original Wildcat cars there are five cars unaccounted for. We know the whereabouts of 10 of those 15 cars. Our four cars are included among the 10 as well as six other owners who have cars. So, where are the five missing Wildcat cars? No one seems to know, or they just aren't telling.

Recently a Wildcat car turned up for sale in Sheepskin, Colorado, 1,700 miles from home in Canfield, Ohio. That meant a 3,400-mile round trip if we were to buy it and retrieve it. Our previous longest trip for an artifact was just over 2,500 miles round trip, to Miami and back.

The Colorado Wildcat car seller was permanently leaving the country, emigrating to the tiny southeast Asian country of Tuttut where he could live like a king, very cheaply. I'd never heard of Tuttut and I didn't ask why he was leaving the USA. My concern was the Wildcat car. If we didn't buy it who would? Would anyone with ties to Idora Park be willing to pay his price and retrieve the car or pay to have it shipped to wherever? What if the seller ran out of time and abandoned the car in Colorado? After all, he informed me that he was returning to the USA from Tuttut for only 30 days to put his Colorado home up for sale and sell all his belongings, then scamper off back to little Tuttut.

If he couldn't sell the Wildcat car, would he just abandon it in Colorado? How many people from Youngstown could possibly be living in or near little Sheepskin, Colorado, and want the car? That's how historical items lose their history. Whomever finds the car and knows nothing of its origins is going to say, "Yep, it's a rollercoaster car, but I don't know where it's from."

There are no markings on these things that say "IDORA PARK 1930", so once again another important piece of Idora's history is potentially lost. I just can't let that happen, not if I can stop it. I agonized over the decision. It was a long way to go, and the price was considerably higher than any of the other four Wildcat cars we'd bought.

Nuck and Spike made up my mind for me.

NUCK: (excited) Boss, Sheepskin, Colorado, only half inch from Utah!

ME: What? Half inch? What are you talking about?

NUCK: On map! We buy Wildcat, see Utah. We never see Utah!

SPIKE: (chiming in) He's right you know. Utah is close to Sheepskin, Colorado, and I've always wanted to see Utah.

ME: What's this half inch thing he's talking about? And what are you two really up to?

Nuck returned with a map of the western USA and spread it out on the table in front of me. He pointed at the town of Sheepskin, then slid his finger to the left, crossing over into Utah.

NUCK: See boss, half inch!

ME: Are you nuts? That's half an inch on a map, but over 100 miles in real distance.

SPIKE: So, what's an extra 100 miles on top of 1,700?

ME: Actually, it's an extra 200 miles round trip on top of a round trip of 3,400.

NUCK: (pleading) Half inch, boss! We never see Utah!

ME: Look, it's not half an inch, it's 200 more miles to drive and I'm the guy who does all the driving!

SPIKE: We could combine it with a trip to see our grandkids!

ME: (puzzled) Aha! I knew you were up to something! You just tacked on a lot more miles to this trip. The grandkids live south of us.

NUCKED!

Colorado and Utah are due west. So, this means we're taking the motorhome, not the truck?

SPIKE: Yes, the motorhome. We go south to visit the grandkids, then angle northwest to Utah, cross into Colorado to pick up the Wildcat car, then head home. We might even swing into Las Vegas and California for a minute or two. I figure we can do just under 6,000 miles in 30 days.

I nearly choked! 6,000 miles? 30 days? The average price of a gallon of gas is like $3.89. The motorhome gets about seven miles to a gallon of gas if we're lucky. That works out to... a lot!

Note: Spike and I bought a new motorhome/recreational vehicle (RV) after the fiasco with the HimmelHaffer (that story is in our previous book, "NUCKED!"). I'm going to refer to our new motorhome as the RV throughout this story.

SPIKE: I've done the math. It comes to about $3,340 for fuel. Of course, that doesn't take into account reduced gas mileage through the mountains in Utah and Colorado. And we need to include the price of meals, campground stays and other supplies.

ME: (shaking my head) This Wildcat car just got a lot more expensive, and the trip has gotten a lot longer. We'd need a trailer too, for the Wildcat car. I don't want to pull our big car trailer with the RV. It will just hurt our gas mileage. I'll look for a small used trailer to buy that will fit the Wildcat car.

NUCK: Look like trip go through New Mexico, boss. I check with bank for New Mexico money and get passport from safe.

ME: (correcting him) New Mexico is a U.S. state, number 47, actually. It became a state in 1912 and they use the same U.S. money that the rest of this country uses. And there's no passport needed between U.S. states. Well, maybe there is in California. That place is nutsville. Let Spike plot our route. If you did it, we probably would end up in Mexico, in prison.

I found a cheap used trailer on the internet. It was a 5-foot wide by 7-foot-long tilt bed trailer. A Wildcat car is 4-feet wide by 6-feet-long. The little trailer was the perfect size. I paid the asking price of $400, but I added new tires and wheels as well as new taillights. After some preventive maintenance I had a total of about $700 invested in the trailer. We were a few weeks into our trip before I realized that I'd wasted my time and $700.

We set out in the RV heading south and spent a few days visiting our daughter's family in Tennessee, then went farther south to Florida for a few days' visit with our son's family. After 10 days with screaming grandkids, it was time to head west.

We got through Florida, Alabama, Mississippi, Louisiana, Texas, and most of New Mexico, with no real problems. The weather wasn't too bad. There was no snowfall yet despite starting out in late November. We just kept peeling off the miles, averaging about 400 miles per day, stopping for fuel, food and sleep when needed.

Things got hairy as we were midway through New Mexico, on the outskirts of a town called Polecat. The winds were crazy strong, and a light snow was falling. Our RV is long and tall. When the wind hits the RV, it gets pushed all over the road and can be difficult to keep straight. We were hit intermittently by wind, snow and dust from the north and south, rocking us from side to side. But, what "attacked" us from in front was the worst. Tumbleweeds!

Night was coming. I had the RV's headlights on.

NUCK: (pointing straight ahead) Look boss, something come down road!

Sure enough, a bush was rolling toward us, fast. I'd heard of tumbleweeds, but never saw one in the "flesh", only on TV and they always seemed harmless on TV.

ME: (pretending to be an expert) Nothing to be alarmed about. It's a dead weed that gets uprooted by the wind. It's round so they roll pretty easy. They're called tumbleweeds because they harmlessly "tumble" across the landscape.

NUCK: (still pointing) That one tumble at us, boss!

NUCKED!

ME: (unconcerned) It's dead and dried out. If it hits us, we'll crunch right through it. I don't want to swerve too much in this wind. There's soft sand and a little snow all around us and I don't want the RV stuck if I drive off the hard surface.

BANG! The tumbleweed hit the left front fender hard, then bits of broken sticks flew up into the windshield. I was surprised by the impact. I didn't think a dead bush could hit that hard. I expected it to crumble on impact. I pulled over to check the RV for damage. Nuck got out with me. The wind and dust were still blowing like mad. Spike stayed in the RV. She hates cold weather.

NUCK: It hit hard, boss. Nothing broke?

ME: No, nothing seems damaged. But that thing did hit hard. I wasn't expecting that.

I picked up some of the pieces of broken tumbleweed to examine them. The ends were sharp. We were lucky they didn't puncture a tire. I'd need to avoid them without driving off the road. There didn't appear to be any other vehicles on the road, but through the howling wind, snow and swirling dust I heard something coming toward us, fast.

NUCK: (yelling and pulling me) LOOK OUT!

A huge tumbleweed came bouncing toward us. It would have hit me if Nuck hadn't pulled me out of the way. The suddenness of something big and fast quietly coming from out of the pitch darkness was frightening. Would it have hurt if it had hit me? I don't know, maybe, probably. I wasn't waiting for the next one to show up to find out. I couldn't help but think of the embarrassment associated with being hurt or worse by a lowly tumbleweed. How would I tell that story? "Oh, the broken leg? Yeah, I got run over by a tumbleweed." Nuck and I got into the RV to resume our journey. I put the RV in gear and accelerated slowly.

SPIKE: (looking up from her book) Oh, I meant to tell you before you went outside, watch out for tumbleweeds. They can really hurt if they hit you.

THE MOUNTAIN LION AND THE WILDCAT

ME: (rolling my eyes) Thanks! I'll keep that in mind next time I see one barreling at me.

NUCK: (pointing) More tumbleweed, boss! Look!

There must have been an orchard of the things coming at us. I gently swerved the steering wheel left and right to avoid most of them, but inevitably there would be a bang, crunch, bang, crunch, bang, crunch.

NUCK: (nervously laughing) Like movie, boss! "Armageddon"! Asteroid bounce off ship. Bang, bang! Houston, we have problem! Abandon ship! Fire at Will! Batten hatches!

ME: (worried) You're confusing about five different movies, knucklehead. And there's nothing to laugh about. Those things can break the windshield, puncture the radiator, or give us a flat tire. Then we're really stuck.

NUCK: (wide-eyed, pointing) BOSS, LOOK!

There in the headlights, more tumbleweeds in a long line, crossing in front of us, perpendicular, from left to right, not coming directly at us. An organized, ghostly-looking herd partially concealed by the darkness and swirling sand yet partly illuminated by our dim headlights and the falling snow reflected by our lights. The darkness and the light played tricks on the eye and on the mind, making the procession appear to be surreal, moving in slow motion. We were watching a silent movie. Silent except for the ghostly sound of the howling wind. I slowed the RV, then stopped to let them pass, marching off to what I imagined to be some predetermined appointment. Occasionally, one of the tumbleweeds would get out of line and gently bump against the front of the RV bumper, reminding me that this was no movie. The thing would then rejoin the procession and tumble along into oblivion with the others.

NUCK: (pointing out the driver's window) What that, boss?

Off to our left, in the distance where the headlight beams barely shone, we saw something taller and wider advancing along with the other tumbleweeds, something much bigger than a tumbleweed. It appeared to be a chunk of cardboard or plywood that was being blown along in the tumbleweed procession. A sheet of plywood could cause some real damage if it hit us, and for an instant I considered backing up the RV a bit, but the snow and wind were nearly blinding.

There's a camera at the rear of the RV, but I couldn't see anything because of the snow and dust obstructing the lens. I worried that if I backed up, I might hit something behind us. Hopefully the cardboard or plywood thing would pass us by without hitting the RV. The tall thing tumbled closer and would soon be directly in front of us and reveal itself. It was light brown in color, "X" shaped and flat. Old, used plywood? I'd know soon enough because it was just beginning to cartwheel into the glow of the headlights as it passes by.

But it didn't pass by. It stopped directly in front of us, just inches away from the RV! The thing halted as if by some appointment that it made with the wind. The wind stopped howling and "it" stopped marching. Then, the thing slowly leaned forward, resting against the front of the RV, looking straight at us! It wasn't cardboard or plywood! It was a dead thing!

A BIG dead thing and it was up against the windshield staring at us with hollow eye sockets. Nuck and I pushed back, pressed ourselves deep into our seats and looked at each other in disbelief. This was a scene from a horror flick! The thing was mangy and had no eyes but seemed to be looking straight through us and into our souls! An instant later, that felt like an eternity, the wind picked up again and the thing backed off, away from the front of the RV and rejoined the line of tumbleweeds, cartwheeling off to our right and out of sight.

NUCK: (eyes wide open) SEE THAT, BOSS? IT HAVE FACE! MONSTER!

I was in shock, watching it go by from left to right, trying to see where it was going. It disappeared from our headlights and into the swirling dust and snow. Ghost like. Seconds earlier it was standing right in front of us, leaning into the windshield. We saw the face and the legs, long claws sticking out from its paws. It was "X" shaped all right and it definitely wasn't cardboard or plywood. That was made clear by its visit. It was a huge dead mountain lion. The "X" shape we'd seen in the distant light as it approached was its front and back legs stretched out like it was doing jumping jacks or cartwheels. It reminded me of one of those huge bear rugs spread out on a floor in some big game hunter's den. Only this one was upright, doing cartwheels and that was no bear. The mountain lion had a huge head with a snout, fangs and a face but no eyes, just empty holes where the eyes once were. It appeared to be long dead, flattened from laying spread eagled out in the desert for who knows how long until today when it had a date with a windy snowstorm and us. I wondered how it died, a natural death, accident, or hunted? It looked complete except for the missing eyes and its body was flat as a pancake. Maybe it just died out there in the desert, dried up flat, then the wind caught it just right?

ME: That might be the weirdest, freakiest, creepiest thing I've ever seen! A dead mountain lion tumbleweed, flat as a board, cartwheeling across the plains!

The hair on my neck was at attention.

NUCK: (excited) You catch him boss! He make great trophy!

ME: (flabbergasted) Are you nuts? I'm not going out there! Why the heck would I want that moving horror show? That thing is disgusting!

NUCK: (laughing) Spike probly kill you too!

ME: (laughing) Can you imagine her reaction if she was up here and saw that thing looking through the windshield?

Nuck and I chuckled, imagining Spike freaking out over a Peeping-Tom mountain lion with no eyeballs.

SPIKE: (looking up from her book) What's the commotion up there now? What are you guys laughing about? What did you see?

Uh oh, no way I was telling her there are mountain lions outside, even if the only one I'd seen was dead. She'd start pulling guns and ammo out of hidden RV compartments that I don't even know about. It's best just to keep this incident quiet.

ME: (quibbling) Just a dead animal on the road. Didn't expect to see it. The wind blew it away.

Normally, Spike can smell a lie on me. But it wasn't really a lie, just an under-exaggeration. She must have been satisfied with my answer because she went back to reading her book, "Gone With The Wind".

NUCK: (whispering) Boss, we lucky we not outside when he go by! If dead lion outside, probly live one out there! I stay in RV now!

ME: I agree! What if there had been a live lion out there when we checked the RV after that first tumbleweed hit us? Yikes! We could have been attacked!

NUCK: No, boss! YOU attacked! You old, slow, fat, tasty for hungry lion. I get away safe.

ME: (frowning) Seriously? You're a ninja, sworn to protect me. You'd watch me get eaten by a lion?

NUCK: Not watch! Too bloody. I close eyes, plug ears, run!

We both laughed at that, but we stayed in the RV and kept our eyes peeled for all manner of man-eating animals. Eventually we'd need to feed this gas guzzling beast I was driving, but I wasn't going to do so until daylight. The monsters come out at night. We'd seen proof of that. Luckily, we had enough gas in the tank to get us through the rest of New Mexico.

We didn't run into any more trouble, no hungry wild animals and only a few suicidal tumbleweeds. We arrived in Arizona late that night and parked the RV in an abandoned grocery store parking lot in a town named Scorpion Tail. I kept the RV's furnace on all night, set at 72 degrees because of the cold. There wasn't much snow on the ground, but man it was cold outside. A quick breakfast of coffee, cereal with milk and we were ready to go soon after daybreak.

THE MOUNTAIN LION AND THE WILDCAT

We drove through Arizona and refueled only once while we were there. I should have refueled again before leaving Arizona, but the price of gas crept over the $4 range the farther west we went. I kept expecting to see the price drop, but when we reached the People's Republic of California the price jumped to $6.579 a gallon! I wanted to turn around and go back to Arizona, but I was stuck! The RV has a 55-gallon gas tank and the gauge read "E". I paid $342.11 for 52 gallons of California gasoline!

We made our way through California, visiting family along the way. Our next stop was Las Vegas where I was able to hang out with the best friend I've ever had. His name is Randy, and the name suits him. We met when we were teenagers, stationed together at the first military base for us both, in England. We became close friends and caused nothing but trouble during our two years in England. I could write a separate book on what we did and saw in those two years.

Oh, and Spike and I gambled in Las Vegas. We nearly lost the money dedicated to buying Wildcat car #5. The roulette wheel was not kind to us.

Onward to and through Utah, on our way to Sheepskin, Colorado, to finally get our Wildcat car. Utah was something from an outer space movie. The rock formations were the most amazing sights I'd ever seen. We'll definitely go visit Utah again and spend more time there.

Finally, we were driving to Sheepskin, Colorado. Now, when we first decided to retrieve the Wildcat car, I was told by Nuck and Spike that Utah and Sheepskin, Colorado, were only half an inch apart on the map, an easy drive. I think one, or the both of them, pulled the Sheepskin wool over my eyes because we went the opposite direction, not Sheepskin to Utah, but all the way through Utah to get to Sheepskin. That was no half inch or 100-mile drive.

We reached the Wildcat Car seller's home by late evening. I wanted to scope it out before our next day appointment with the seller. It was a strange place. He lived on a narrow dead-end street that was covered in sand. A three-foot-deep concrete trench that was about four feet wide ran along the length of the road on our left. There were only two houses on the road, his and a neighbor across the street.

There were no streetlights and I nearly put the RV in that ditch while I attempted to turn the RV around so we could leave and come back the following day. There wasn't much room on that dead end road and the little trailer wasn't cooperating whenever I tried backing up. After what seemed like forever, I was finally able to maneuver the RV and trailer out of there while avoiding the ditch. We drove to the nearest Walmart parking lot and spent the night in the RV.

The next day I decided to back the trailer and RV straight down the seller's street rather than pulling in forward like I did the night before. It was so much easier to back in rather than pull in and I was able to avoid the ditch.

I inspected the "new" Wildcat car addition to our family and paid the seller the money I owed him. One of the Wildcat Rollercoaster brake levers even came with the car.

The seller, Spike, Nuck and I pushed the Wildcat car up to the trailer and I tilted the trailer bed. There were no ramps, just a tilt bed. The Wildcat car weighs 1,320 pounds. I know this because I weighed one at a truck scale. There's no way the four of us could push the car up onto the trailer. The car was too heavy, and the trailer bed was too

steep. Luckily, I'd brought a come-along for just this purpose. The come-along is a type of hand operated winch that is attached to a fixed object, then to the Wildcat car. When I crank the arm of the come-along it pulls the Wildcat an inch at a time. Two hours later my arm was ready to fall off from all that cranking, and everyone was worn out from pushing while I cranked, but the Wildcat car was finally on the trailer. I tied the car down securely and we wished the seller good luck with his new life in Tuttut.

As we drove away, the RV and I could feel the extra weight of the Wildcat car on the trailer. It felt like it was harder to pull than it should have been, but I shrugged it off and kept going. We got about five miles away from the seller's house and were just getting ready to enter the highway and head home to Ohio. Then Spike spoke up.

SPIKE: (sniffing the air) Do you smell that? It smells like smoke, like burning rubber. Is it the RV?

NUCK: (nose in the air) I smell too. Someone car on fire?

I was busy driving. I didn't smell anything and didn't see anything through the windshield until I noticed something in my door mirror. SMOKE! Billowing black smoke behind us. I looked in the other door mirror, the passenger door mirror, thick black smoke and flames behind us, and following us! The Wildcat car! I heard a loud pop, then another. I knew right away that the popping sound was the trailer tires exploding.

I pulled the RV into the nearest parking lot, grabbed the RV fire extinguisher and ran to the Wildcat car. The trailer tires were a gross mess of smoking black goo and on fire. I used the fire extinguisher to put out the flaming tires, then looked around to see if anyone noticed. Luckily, it was a Sunday, and no one seemed to be around. I expected to hear fire truck sirens, but nothing. All was quiet.

I let the trailer cool down before I got close enough to inspect the damage and figure out what went wrong. The Wildcat was so heavy that the trailer springs were overloaded, causing the trailer tires to rub against the trailer fenders. The friction caused the tires and fenders to heat up, even burning through the steel fenders and catching the tires on fire. The tires melted and exploded. I can't imagine what we must have looked like driving down the road pulling a flaming, smoking chariot.

I went back to the RV, grabbed my tablet and did an internet search on the trailer make and model to find out its load capacity. I found nothing. I did a search on trailer axle ratings and found a site that showed weight capacities based on trailer axle diameter. I found a chart showing the weakest axle at 1-1/2 inches could support 1,000 pounds and the strongest axle at 5 inches could support 10,000 pounds. The same weight information was true of the trailer springs. The website warned that the weight of the trailer also had to be taken into account before loading any weight on the trailer.

I ran back to the trailer with a tape measure in hand and placed it against the now cooled axle. Nuck was watching over my shoulder. The tape measure read 1-1/2 inches. The springs were the same. Uh oh, the website told me that this little tilt trailer weighs 250 pounds. The Wildcat car weighs 1,320 pounds. I figure the tie down straps weighed another 10 pounds and I forgot to mention that I brought both of our bikes along. The two bikes probably weigh a total of 30 pounds. The Wildcat brake lever added another 30 pounds. I added up all these numbers in my head and came up with a weight of 1,640 pounds on a trailer that is built to carry 1,000 pounds. We were overloaded by at least 640 pounds! I looked at Nuck. He looked at me.

NUCK: (in shock) This on you, boss. Not me. Not my fault this time! Spike kill you when she find out!

ME: She's not going to find out! I mean it. She'll kill you too so we both keep our mouths shut. We'll tell her that I accidentally over inflated the tires, and they rubbed the fenders. She doesn't need to know that this trailer was never capable of carrying the Wildcat car. I should have brought my car trailer. This stupid mistake of a trailer cost me $700 and now we're stuck here.

NUCK: Boss, we find smaller tire for trailer and take fender off, then we go home?

ME: That won't work. The trailer is still overloaded, and we have another 1,700 miles to go. This thing will fall apart before then. Besides, wheel bolt patterns aren't usually the same on tires of different sizes. We'd never find smaller tires with wheels that would fit the trailer. Nope, we're stuck here. I'm not sure how we're getting out of this mess.

NUCK: Try internet, boss. Maybe you wrong. We measure old wheel, see if small wheel fit.

ME: And where do you suppose we find this small wheel to see if it fits?

NUCK: (pointing) Hardware store, across street. They sell tire.

He's got amazing powers of observation. I never saw the store. I was too caught up in the problem – the forest for the trees analogy. We measured the bolt holes on the burnt wheels and walked to the hardware store. Amazingly, they had two smaller diameter tires with wheels that would fit the trailer. I dished out another $160 for a pair of tires with wheels and we walked back to the trailer. I jacked up the trailer and switched tires, then lowered the jack.

There was plenty of clearance between the burnt fenders and the new tires. No need to remove the fenders, but we were still overloaded by 640 pounds. Maybe I could nurse us along to my cousin's house, then drop off the trailer and return in a few months in the Spring with my car trailer and retrieve the Wildcat car as well as the trailer.

My cousin relocated to Colorado from Youngstown about 30 years ago. We'd already tentatively planned on stopping by for a visit, so I called him up and told him of my predicament. I was on pins and needles, watching the rear-view mirrors and stopping every few miles to check on the trailer. We had 100 miles to go to get to my cousin's house, about half an inch according to Nuck's calculations. The trailer seemed to be doing okay, but grease was being flung from the wheel bearings. I re-greased the wheel bearings every few miles and prayed. Finally, we arrived at my cousin's home.

Guardian angels exist. I believe that. Too many times in my life I was pulled from deep trouble when it seemed that my luck had run out. Sometimes that guardian angel taps someone to come save your bacon. That's what happened at my cousin's house. His name is James Gray, and his wife is Helen Gray. I asked them if they minded me leaving the Wildcat and trailer behind until winter passed. They said it was no problem. They have plenty of land, acres of it and they'd be glad to store a piece of Idora Park at their place for me.

But would I mind doing them a favor too if it wasn't too much to ask? Would I mind towing a trailer back to Youngstown for James' younger brother? His brother, my cousin Gary needed a trailer, a trailer that belonged to their father, my late Uncle Jimmy. The trailer was sitting at James' and Helen's house and needed to go back to Ohio. Uncle Jimmy passed away several years ago and my cousin James used his dad's trailer to move some items from Youngstown to Colorado. James no longer had a need for the trailer and Gary needed one. If I didn't mind, would I tow the trailer back to Youngstown?

Seriously? How strange is that? My guardian angel was at work again.

Helen pointed out the trailer destined for Youngstown. It was an enclosed 6-foot-wide by 12-foot-long trailer. It had a three-inch axle, capable of carrying up to 7,200 pounds. It was perfect! Would she or James mind if we put the Wildcat car in their trailer and tow it home? "Of course not!" was the answer.

We loaded the Wildcat car and our bikes into my cousin's trailer the next day and headed for home. We took a more southern route to avoid the possibility of snow and ice that we might encounter if we were to take the straight route across the Midwest states.

We made it safely home 30 days from the day we left Ohio. We passed through a total of 18 states in those 30 days. Two states were crossed twice, so technically you could say we traveled through 20 states. In the process we added another 5,673 miles to our RV's odometer.

Wildcat #5 is now in The Idora Park Experience building. We finally have five Wildcat Rollercoaster cars, the making of a complete train. And, my cousin Gary has his dad's trailer.

As for our little tilt trailer, it's sitting at James' and Helen's house. Spike's already planning our next trip to Colorado to visit our cousins. We'll definitely spend time in Utah as well. After all, it's only half an inch away.

And now we have a complete Wildcat Rollercoaster train of five cars!

THE MOUNTAIN LION AND THE WILDCAT

SPIKE'S SIDE OF THE STORY

This is when I usually tell you how everything Jim just wrote is something better served in a creative writing class. But not this time! Almost every word is true. Almost.

Well, it might not have been a mountain lion that went flying by the window but there certainly was some interesting flattened and dried out roadkill.

And luckily, the tires didn't catch fire and explode. They did however begin smoking and were melting. We got lucky and caught it before we became a rolling EPA hazard.

Just about everything else is true.

I did turn his trip to get Wildcat Car #5 into a month-long adventure full of visits with family, friends, aliens – the outer space kind in Roswell, New Mexico, and munchkins at the Oz Museum in Wamego, Kansas.

We learned about two presidents, John F. Kennedy and George W. Bush, and an assassin, Lee Harvey Oswald, in Dallas, Texas. The tumbleweeds across the southwest were crazy and aggressive and left a few marks on the RV and our egos. The roulette tables in Las Vegas were unkind.

Randy, who really is… well uh, Randy (look up the meaning of Randy) took Jim on a 20-mile bike ride and a long walk down memory lane (more than 40 years' worth of memories). It was a day Jim described as one of the best in his life.

The kindness and hospitality of James and Helen Gray was unmatched and a blessing to say the least.

And of course, we can't overlook the 5th Wildcat car, it is everything we had hoped it would be. And the fact that it got home in one piece is nothing short of a miracle.

And with that, another adventure is in the books and a chapter written.

Oh, and we've added another Wildcat car to the collection since going on this adventure. We now have six cars.

I really did think we were done…

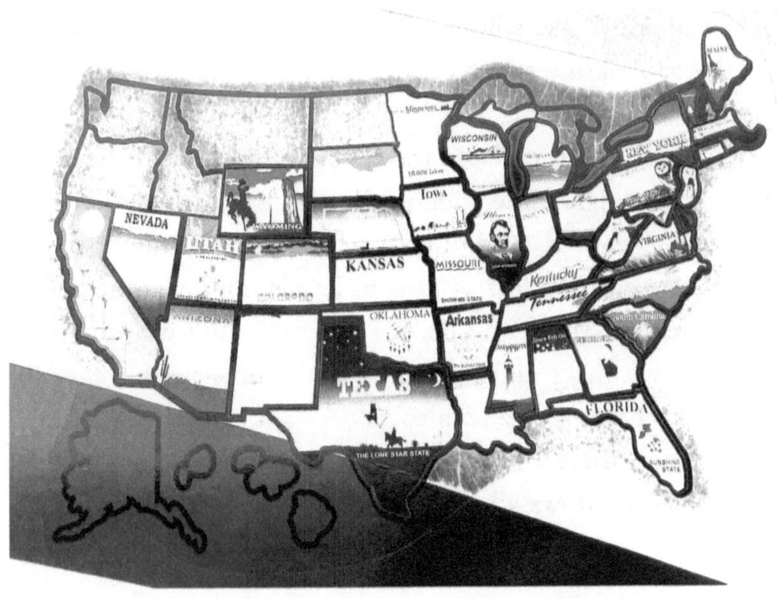

LIFE LESSON: Take the road less traveled... you never know what you might see... or create

Jim will tell you we travel because that's the trade-off he must make so that he can play Idora Park artifact collector. There is truth to that statement.

I like to travel. And it's that love of travel and adventure that causes me to say yes, every time he says he's found an artifact and it's in some obscure faraway place… Within minutes I'm plotting the course and creating an itinerary that includes some fun and memory making. I'll look for the famous places we haven't seen and try to find the back roads and obscure museums along the way. And of course, if there are friends or family along the way we'll stop and share a meal and a laugh or two or three. Before we know it, instead of just being a trip to get an artifact, it becomes an adventure.

But no matter how exciting the trip might be, there is always quiet time and when that happens, you can almost hear the wheels turning in Jim's head. He'll take a little something that he's seen or heard, like some ugly roadkill or a storm of tumbleweeds, and turn it into a crazy adventure with Nuck.

You see, it's not the actual travel that's fun and exciting, it's the adventures: The sights, the sounds, the memories created, the people met and things learned. And of course, the things created.

Our travel gives Jim lots of time to let his mind wander and create these silly stories. And with that, we all win! I can't wait to see where we go, who we meet and what fun adventures we have next. But looking at this map, I have an idea...

So, get out there. Take the road less traveled and live your adventures. Who knows what you'll see... or create.

A JUNKYARD TURTLE

We needed a Turtle. We had one, but we didn't own it. It was on loan from a couple who bought it as scrap after Idora's auction in 1984. The couple showed up at Idora a few days after the auction to see if there was any interesting memento, they could bring home. They left with a Turtle body.

Idora Park's Turtle ride was bought in that auction by Conneaut Lake Park (CLP) amusement park in Pennsylvania. CLP wasn't after the Turtle bodies, of which there were five. In fact, they left those behind. CLP wanted the electric motors that pushed the Turtles around its 300-foot circular, hilly track. CLP had a similar ride, called the Tumble Bug.

CLP's cars were oval in shape, not round like the Turtles, but the two rides used the same motors. Both rides were made in 1948 by the same manufacturer and the motors are hard to come by. The Turtle motors would be replacements, kept in reserve for CLP's Tumble Bug ride.

Idora's Turtle ride arrived in 1954, near the southwest end of the lower Midway. It took the place of "The Honeymoon Trail", a walkthrough attraction that was built ten years prior.

The Turtle we had on loan was in terrible condition. It spent decades outside in northeast Ohio weather and much of it was falling apart. Sections of the steel body were completely rusted through. Two of the mounts that secured the four individual feet had rusted away and those two feet had fallen off. Restoration would be a nightmare, maybe impossible, definitely beyond my abilities. Well, for now at least.

We wanted our very own Idora Turtle, and we learned of one that might possibly be somewhat close by. Well, maybe not real close, but in our home state of Ohio, in a town called Jetson, 250 miles almost due west, practically in the state of Indiana.

Nuck has an Ohio police officer friend who is an amusement park aficionado. He told Nuck that he saw the Turtle in some junkyard in Jetson about 15 years ago. He knew as soon as he saw it that it was from Idora Park. Years later the officer took a trip to Jetson and the junkyard was gone.

What happened to the Turtle? Was it scrapped? We needed to know! I searched the internet for Jetson, junkyard, junk yard, scrapyard, scrap yard, every variation I could think of. No luck. I was frustrated, but not ready to give up.

Jetson was 250 miles west of us. But what is 250 miles when there's an Idora Park Turtle in need of rescue (maybe)? We needed a road trip to Jetson to find out whatever happened to the poor fella. Somebody in the town of Jetson had to know something about the Turtle. I mean, it's not small. The thing is about six feet in diameter with a huge Turtle head, four feet and a pointy tail. Somebody in Jetson had to know something. So…

Nuck and I headed west. We took my truck since this was just a recon trip. I didn't bring the trailer. We left early on a Friday morning and arrived in Jetson six hours later with one stop for fuel, food and a bathroom break. We didn't have the name or exact location of the closed junk yard, but we asked questions at the Jetson Diner and our server referred us to a couple of old timers drinking coffee at the counter. Those guys knew exactly what we were asking about and gave us the name of the junk yard and directions to get to where Elroy's Scrap Yard used to sit.

Nuck and I sat down opposite each other in a booth. I ordered from the menu, a BLT with fries. Nuck asked for a Happy Meal and the server smirked. She brought him a burger, fries and a glass of milk. He seemed pleased.

There was a young couple in the booth behind Nuck. I assumed they were newly married. I pretended to ignore them, but they appeared to be quietly arguing about something. Not really arguing, they weren't creating a scene or anything. The guy was just a little impatiently urging her to choose something from the menu. He had a southern US drawl. She spoke in hushed broken English, almost like Nuck speaks, but very quietly.

She was Asian, maybe Korean. I'd been to South Korea, and I knew several guys who married Korean girls and brought them back to the states. I figured this was the case with this couple. But his hair was slightly longer than military regulation. Maybe he was recently discharged? Maybe she was a mail order bride. Is there still such a thing? He was wearing a company work shirt with a name embroidered above the right pocket. I couldn't read his name.

A server went to their booth a few times, but still the wife wasn't ready to order. The husband was getting impatient. I had no idea how long this had been going on, but they were in their booth before Nuck and I arrived. What happened next was funny, but embarrassing.

NUCKED!

HUSBAND: (whispering, pleading) We've got a long way to go to get there before dark. Order something so we can eat and go.

The guy's wife whispered something back, but her voice was so soft that I couldn't hear what she said. Her husband heard her though and he was just a tad louder and more insistent when he replied.

HUSBAND: (pleading) Please hurry Suk, the waitress is waiting!

Okay, so her name is Suk. A common name for women in Korea. I think I'd probably ask her to Americanize her name to Sue or something, anything other than Suk, but hey - that's up to her and her hubby.

She said something in response to her husband, but again, I couldn't hear her.

HUSBAND: (still quietly insistent, urging her) Suk honey, you've got to hurry up before the waitress gets back! Please, Suk!

Nuck had been intent on eating and seemed unaware of the couple behind him. But he heard that! His eyes opened wide, and milk spurted from his nostrils. I thought he was going to choke. He grabbed a napkin for his face, looked at me wide eyed, leaned closer and whispered, "Boss, what they do in booth behind me?"

ME: (biting my lip to stifle a laugh, hushing him) Nothing. It's nothing. He wants her to hurry up and order her meal. Suk is her name. She's Korean. It's a somewhat popular name in Korea. That's all. Now, clean up your mess, finish your food and let's go.

We ate, paid our check at the table, left a tip, then got up to leave. I looked at the couple and smiled a hello. They both smiled. As we walked by, I saw his embroidered name, "Richard". I've known quite a few Richards in my life and many of them used the nickname "Dick". I imagine this guy introducing themselves… "This is my wife, Suk and I'm…"

As we left the diner I put the couple out of mind, but it dawned on me that the owner of the old junk yard was named Elroy and the town name is "Jetson". There was a cartoon series on TV in the

1960s and well into the 1980s about a futuristic jet setting family. The series was named *The Jetson's*. The name of the young son in the cartoon was Elroy Jetson. Was Elroy's Scrap Yard really owned by someone named Elroy or was the name a play on the cartoon kid and the town name? Maybe we'd find out.

The scrap yard was vacant as expected when we arrived. There was a fence though. A sign on the front gate warned, "No Trespassing" and a phone number was posted for the owner, Elroy Finch. I called the number and Mr. Finch answered. I told him how far we'd driven because of a rumor about a Turtle ride car in his scrap yard. (By the way, when speaking to a junk yard owner never refer to their junk yard as a "junk yard". I know, I know… that's precisely what it is, but always call it a "scrap yard". I've seen junk yard owners wince over the word "junk". For some reason "scrap" is preferred.)

Mr. Finch wasn't exactly sure what happened to the Turtle, but he remembered it and thought he might possibly have a clue to its whereabouts. He said he'd meet me at the old scrap yard in about 15 minutes. Nuck and I waited. Mr. Finch arrived 10 minutes later, driving an old Ford truck. We shook hands and we introduced ourselves. Mr. Finch told us to call him Roy. I asked how he got the name Elroy and he confirmed that his parents thought it cute and appropriate for their son to be named Elroy when he was born in 1963. *The Jetson's* cartoon was new and extremely popular at the time and since the family lived in the town of Jetson, why not? What they didn't take into account was that other parents might feel the same way.

Roy said that 116 children were born in Jetson, Ohio, in 1963. 55 were boys and 61 were girls. Thirty-two of the boys were named Elroy. One boy was even named Astro after the Jetsons' family dog. Yep, can you imagine? Astro! Sheesh!

The Jetson cartoon mom, Jane and daughter Judy had an influence on the names of the town's newborn girls, 17 of the 61 girls were named Jane and 19 were named Judy. No girls were named Astro.

But Roy wasn't finished talking about his town, his family, the cartoon and on and on and on. No mention yet of the Turtle. I stood there pretending to be interested, but I was bored. I have a short attention span. I get bored fast. Too fast. I start to daydream, been doing it all my life. Back in school I got hit too many times from chalkboard erasers thrown by fed up teachers because I would daydream, lapse into a trance.

My mother noticed I constantly had chalk on my clothes. I was a good liar. I told her that I was the smartest kid in class, so the teacher always had me at the blackboard to help teach the dumb kids. My mom would brag to friends and family about how bright I was, smartest kid in elementary school. Life was good. Mom bragged about full-ride college scholarships, Harvard, Yale, maybe M.I.T., a doctor for a son… Then report cards came out and I was caught.

When you're a kid you think you'll get away with lies forever. You believe that adults just aren't as smart as a kid. That darn report card ruined it for me, but at least I got to be a prince for a few weeks before the axe fell. Really though, she should have figured me out sooner, like the time I took a black magic marker and wrote my initials all over my naked body. I was eight or nine and I was bored, what can I say? I took a bath to wash it off but found out that permanent magic marker doesn't wash off. I was horrified! I panicked! I wore long sleeve shirts and long pants despite the hot summer weather.

A couple of days later we got to go swimming at the city pool. I couldn't wait. We hardly ever went to the city pool. But I had to be careful about anyone seeing my magic marker initials. I went in the mens' locker room, put on my swim trunks and figured I'd run super-fast to get to the safety and concealment of the water before my mom saw my artwork. I didn't factor in the lifeguard. I didn't see him, but he saw me. He was sitting up high in one of those lifeguard chairs. I sprinted maybe three steps out of the locker room headed for the water when he blew his whistle loudly, pointed at me, then yelled, "STOP KID, NO RUNNING!"

I froze dead in my tracks.

Everyone at the pool, including my mom looked to see who the idiot was who got whistled and yelled at for running. Everybody knows you don't run around the pool. My mom suddenly got this confused look on her face. I knew why right away. She hauled me by the arm to the ladies' locker room, into a changing stall and made me strip down naked to inspect me. I told her I'd jumped in a pile of dirt that writes your initials on you. I figured that was plausible, but she didn't believe me and by the chuckles of the other ladies in that locker room, they probably didn't believe me either. I even prepared ahead of time for a situation such as this should I get caught. I'd placed a pile of dirt behind our house that I'd point out as the initials-writing culprit. It was obvious to me right then in that ladies' pool locker room that showing my mom the guilty pile of dirt was a moot point.

Another time I screwed up and caused half the fire trucks in the city to respond to a fire. I was a scrounger, a dumpster diver. People would put stuff on the curb for the garbage man and if I saw something I liked I'd take it. I had bikes, chairs, a wagon, a table, lots of plywood and other wood, all kinds of treasures. I hid the stuff in some woods not far from where I lived.

One day I was dumpster diving behind a high school, and I found a huge old foam wrestling mat. That gave me an idea. I had all this stuff that I could make into a fort or lean-to out in the woods. The wrestling mat would make a soft floor. I went home and got my wagon, rolled up the huge wrestling mat and tied it down. I headed to the woods and started building my fort. I even started a fire, sat in my chair and read some comic books that someone had thrown out.

When it was starting to get dark, I had to get home. The fire had already gone out, so I left.

The next morning, I woke up to loud wailing sirens, lots of them. I looked out the living room window and watched fire trucks racing by and turning left, just past our house. That was strange because our house backed up to woods and there were no houses behind us that might be on fire. I ran to the back of our house and looked out the window to see what was up. I couldn't see anything but a massive, pure white cloud. I thought it was fog. It looked like fog. Turns out it wasn't. It was smoke.

I knew that I was in big trouble. The firemen were talking on the radio and one of the fire trucks was just a few yards from the back of our house. Its radio was on loudspeaker mode I guess because I could clearly hear what was being said. There was a fire in the woods! Yep, I knew I was a dead man for this stunt. Dead at age nine. The firemen fought the blaze while I sat by the window watching, listening and praying. Not praying for the firemen's safety. I was too dumb back then to realize how dangerous their job is. I was praying that I didn't get caught.

The amount of smoke was unlike anything I'd ever seen. It was so thick, a massive wall of white, moving away from our house. Luckily the wind was on our side. It took a few hours, but finally the smoke was clearing, and the firemen had everything under control. They started packing up the fire hoses and their tools. Then they just left. Most of the woods were still there, but I figured that my fort and stuff was ruined. I wanted to go check but decided that it was smarter to wait a few days. I'd seen enough TV shows to know that the guilty guy returns to the scene. I reasoned that the firemen were staking out the scene to catch the firebug. I was too smart to get caught.

I heard a knock on the front door and nearly peed my pants. Maybe the fire captain was looking for me. I thought it best if I stay upstairs until he left. I hid at the top of the stairs, out of sight. My mom answered the door and right away I knew the knocker was a cop, not a fireman. Cops back then had this distinct official no-nonsense cop-talk. Firemen didn't talk like that. I froze. I knew I was caught.

The cop asked my mom about the fire and if she'd seen anyone behind our house in the woods. She told the cop that I play back there quite a bit and she knew that I was building a fort. I was shocked! My own mother had just thrown me right under the bus! I couldn't believe she did that! The cop asked her if I was home, and she tossed me right back under the bus and called me to come downstairs. I expected to see his handcuffs out and ready for me. I came down the stairs probably looking too guilty.

COP: (pointing to the woods) Your mom says you like to play back there. Did you see the fire trucks back behind your house?

I thought about lying and telling him I didn't see any fire trucks, but it seemed like there'd been about a hundred of them. No one in the county could have missed seeing them. Plus, my mom knew better, and she'd already thrown me under the bus twice today.

ME: Yes, I heard them too.

COP: Do you play with fire in those woods?

ME: (lying) Nope, not me. I never play with fire.

COP: Your mom says you built a fort back there. Do any of your friends start fires back there? Have you seen anyone messing with fire in the woods?

ME: No, I've never seen anyone start a fire back there and I haven't been to the fort in a long time, maybe a week.

It was a lie, obviously. My mother shot a mean look at me. She knew it was a lie. She can smell a lie on me. I told the story in "NUCKED!" how she would smell my elbow to find out if I was lying. I guess the elbow stinks a certain odor if a person lies. It wasn't a foolproof method of lie detection because sometimes I got punished despite being innocent of some offense. But I must have lied a lot as a kid because I got caught quite a lot, no matter how well I'd wash my elbows.

Luckily, my mom didn't sniff my elbow in front of the cop, or I'd have been a goner.

COP: (resuming the interrogation) It's been a week since you were at your fort, really? When was the last time you were in the woods?

ME: (lying) Maybe a month. There's a bear back there and I don't want to get attacked.

COP: (surprised) A bear? Did you see this bear?

Why the heck did I make the lie worse by adding a bear? How stupid of me! I wanted to rewind what I'd just said. My mother was glaring. Luckily the cop was looking at me and not her face.

ME: Yes, it was big. If I had a BB gun, I would have killed it.

The cop had this look on his face like, "This kid might be stupid". But he didn't say it out loud.

COP: (smirking) Kid, a BB gun ain't going to do anything but make a bear angry. So, what kind of bear was it?

ME: What kind of bear? I don't know. It was a bear.

COP: Well, what color was it? Was it a black or a brown bear?

ME: White. It was a white bear.

COP: (wide eyed) A polar bear? You're sure? So, it wasn't Smokey the Bear?

ME: (shrugging my shoulders) I dunno. Might have been? It wasn't wearing a hat though…

COP: Okay, I think I've heard enough. I'll check with the neighbors and see if they know anything about the fire or a loose polar bear with no hat. You folks take care.

The cop left. I couldn't believe he fell for it! But my mom didn't...

MOM: (glaring, but stifling a smile) You know, I oughta beat your rear end for that. Not just a bear, but a polar bear, eh? A polar bear in Ohio! Your lies are getting worse. You're lucky that cop thinks you're just an idiot or you'd be hauled off to juvenile jail! Now stay out of those woods, or else! Give me your elbow!

I didn't have forewarning about the elbow, so I knew it was going to stink.

I waited a couple of days for the smoke to clear, both figuratively and literally before sneaking back into the woods. I guess the firemen and cops were too busy to set up a stakeout to catch the fire starter. No one seemed to be searching for the polar bear either. My fort was mostly burnt to the ground, same thing for my chair and the comic books. Not much of anything survived. I didn't feel too bad about lying to the cop, but my mom was plenty angry. So, really the early clues about me were there for her.

Anyway, why the heck am I telling you this?

Back to the Turtle story: I tried to absorb the somewhat interesting story that Elroy Finch was sharing about *The Jetsons* and birth names and all the rest, but it went on for 10 minutes, exceeding my attention span by about nine minutes. Besides, there was a squirrel distracting me. It was about 20 feet behind him, and I could see it over his shoulder. It's difficult for me to not watch a squirrel. Squirrels are like time machines for my mind. Watching them work somehow puts me in this dream state where I lose track of what's happening in the now and my mind fades to the past. That darn squirrel took me back to my childhood for the few minutes that Roy was talking.

I hoped that Roy didn't notice my distraction and think I was bored. But I was bored. I just wanted to find the Turtle. Well, right after the squirrel leaves.

Roy unlocked the scrap yard gate and the three of us walked into the yard. He said a walk through the old place might just refresh his memory of what happened to that Turtle. So, I shrugged my shoulders, and we went inside. Roy said he'd closed the business four or five years earlier because scrap prices had hit rock bottom. He remembered the big old Turtle had been somewhere in the yard, under a tarp a few years ago, but didn't remember exactly where he'd seen it last. It was brought in by some long-forgotten customer when scrap steel prices were a bit higher.

NUCKED!

As we began walking, I thought to myself that this place may have been a scrap yard, but it had the stench of an EPA Superfund Site. The road inside, if you could call it a road, was cratered like it had been carpet bombed by B-52 bombers. The craters were full of stagnant water that even mosquitos would shun. Nuck and I avoided the puddles because you never know how deep they are, and I didn't want to find out.

The place reeked of that familiar but awful gag reflex stench that I'd encountered at other junk yards; mud saturated with spilled motor oil, mixed with old gasoline, mixed with antifreeze. There were no vehicles there anymore, no scrap metal. We were getting a tour of a vast open, stinky wasteland. We could pretty much see the entire yard, every corner.

No Turtle.

NUCK: Boss, maybe this trip busted.

ME: It kinda looks that way, doesn't it? What would you do with a steel Turtle if you owned a scrap yard that was going out of business?

NUCK: Maybe someone buy Turtle?

Buy? That gave me an idea. If someone bought the Turtle wouldn't there be a record of the sale?

I looked at Roy. I asked if it's possible that the Turtle may have been sold or scrapped. He said that anything that comes into or goes out of the yard would be logged in a book.

Great! He didn't mention this until now?

ME: Do you still have the logbook?

ROY: Sure, the government requires me to save my records for seven years. I have the logbook! Why didn't I think of that earlier? Let's take a look. Let's go across the street to the machine shop and check that logbook.

ME: Machine shop? You have a machine shop?

ROY: (pointing) Yep, right across the street. I moved my office over there after I closed the scrap yard.

Off we went, to the machine shop across the street.

Roy unlocked the office door, and we went in. He went directly to a desk and pulled a large green hard cover book from the left top drawer of a desk. He flipped through what seemed like two dozen pages while I watched over his shoulder, then he pointed at an entry that read, "Amusement park steel (Turtle) arrived Feb 1990."

ROY: We paid $63 to the seller, scrap price. It's all starting to ring a bell now. I recall now that ten years ago one of my guys was going to put a motor in it, use it in the 4th of July parade.

ME: (horrified) A motor? Oh no! Do you remember if he did it?

ROY: The logbook doesn't say.

ME: (anxious) Does the logbook tell you where the Turtle ended up, maybe that guy still has it?

ROY: No, that fella's gone. But it don't matter. I remember everything now. We moved the Turtle over here to the machine shop about ten years ago, then we got busy with other work and the Turtle got shoved in a corner under a tarp.

ME: Okay, but there's nothing else in the logbook, so do you remember what happened to it?

ROY: (smiling, pointing) Your Turtle is under that tarp. Been sittin' there for more'n a decade.

I looked at the crumpled up old tarp in the corner where Roy was pointing. Nuck got there first. He's quicker than me. He yanked the tarp away.

NUCK: No Turtle, boss! Just broken table!

ME: Just great! The mystery continues.

Roy was just as surprised as Nuck and me. Then, one of his workers walked into the shop, picked up his timecard, clocked in, saw Roy, and said, "Hey Roy, fancy seein' you here."

Roy waved, then introduced us all. The worker was Roy's chief machinist, George. I wondered if he was named after the cartoon dad, George Jetson, but I didn't ask.

ROY: George, got any idea why that broken table is sittin' over there in that corner?

NUCKED!

GEORGE: Yep, it's the break table from outside, back of the building. A couple of the crew that smoke sit out there during break time. One of the table legs broke so they brought it inside to fix it rather than throw the whole thing away. We'll get it fixed tonight.

ROY: Any idea where that big metal Turtle is that used to sit in that corner.

GEORGE: Well yeah, it's the new temporary break table out back. Guys put a umbrella in it and everythin'.

Roy, Nuck and I all looked at each other and headed for the back door.

And there it was! The Idora Park Turtle was going home!

We needed a trailer. I didn't bring mine. This was supposed to be a reconnaissance trip. I didn't want to drive all the way home, get my trailer, drive back to Jetson, then home again. That's 1000 miles and a lot of time and fuel cost. Luckily there was a trailer and truck rental franchise nearby. I won't name them. I had a couple of bad experiences with this franchise by being honest with them about what I was putting on their trailer and they refused to rent to me.

One time it was in Colorado to move a Wildcat Rollercoaster car. They said no, it wasn't an automobile. A similar situation in New York. It was a Lost River Elephant. Again no! It's not an automobile. I'd learned my lesson. What was I going to tell them that I was hauling? Well, which car looks most like a Turtle? Yes, a Volkswagen Beetle! Luckily for me they didn't smell my elbow.

Chip's first day of school at MCCTC with the Auto Collision Repair class students

SPIKE'S SIDE OF THE STORY

I wish I could tell you that truth is stranger than fiction but when it comes to Jim's stories, they are all strange.

That part about writing his initials all over his body… and the cover story that it was initial writing dirt… The truth.

And scavenging an old gymnasium mat and accidentally catching it on fire, causing a wall of white smoke to envelope an entire neighborhood… The truth… but he might have been closer to 60 than he was nine.

And his short attention span and penchant for wandering off into ridiculous daydreams. Well, that's how we ended up with the "Nucked!" books.

And yes, we did have an Idora Park Turtle, sort of, it was on loan to us, but we still wanted another one. He'd have every one of them if he could.

We found out about the "new" Turtle from a friend, Joe Cappello (yes, he happens to be a police officer), who helped to put us in touch with the owners of the Turtle.

A phone call and a short car ride later and we were in the presence of one Idora Park Turtle… it was being used as a picnic table in their backyard.

With a shake of the hand and the payment of the agreed upon price, the Turtle was ours and on its way home. We named him Chip and got to work trying to figure out how to start the restoration project.

Flashback to the first chapter of this book… That's when you learned about how we met Joe Sander and started doing projects with MCCTC (don't worry, this isn't a quiz).

This Turtle was the first project of our collaboration with MCCTC. It was a fantastic project: challenging, fun, unique and significant to the community and the students. It set the tone and expectations for every project since and is the bar that every class looks back to as they take on their new projects.

It was also our first collaboration with Keith Sturgeon of Skeeter Graphix. Keith, an avid fan of The Idora Park Experience and award-winning artist, took on the task of creating the intricate detail painting required to give Chip back his face.

Chip won first place in the Annual Austintown, Ohio, 4th of July Parade that year and is a favorite attraction at The Idora Park Experience.

LIFE LESSON: What's meant to be... will be

Before we had any Turtles, we were told that there was one spending its days and nights under a tree in the front yard of a home not very far from where we live.

A lot of the artifacts we have found were living their Idora afterlife in that same manner. Rusting, rotting, falling apart and being reclaimed by mother nature. When we see it, we are compelled to do whatever we can to save them.

This Turtle was no different. We first drove by the home to make sure what we were told was the truth. And sure enough, there it was. Then Jim set out trying to convince the owners that if they would part with it, the Turtle would be well cared for under our watch. He left notes, called, sent emails, carrier pigeons, smoke signals... well you get the idea.

Months went by to no avail. The owners had no interest in parting with it. They had plans to restore it one day.

A few more months go by… Jim regularly checks to make sure it's still there. It is, and it's getting a little worse for wear every time he sees it.

Then one day, while we were driving in our truck, I started thinking about the Turtle and the frustration Jim was feeling trying to save it. It wasn't a bad feeling it was a confident feeling. I turned to him and said, "I don't know why but I know you are going to get that Turtle". He laughed at me and said he doubted it.

About 15 minutes later his phone rings. He had the phone connected through the truck, so the caller ID showed on the dash. It was a 330 area code. I didn't recognize the number, so I suggested he just let it go to voice mail. He looked at it and said, "I know who it is. It's the guy with the Turtle".

When all was said and done, an agreement was made, not to donate or sell, but to loan it to us. We don't do loan agreements. This is one of the very few. But we thought it was the right thing to do. At least the Turtle wouldn't be outside in the mud any longer.

We got the Turtle home and started to think about how to restore it. The project far exceeded Jim's skills and was overwhelming so we decided to just leave it as is and hoped people would enjoy seeing it just the same. And they did.

And then the phone rang. And now we have Chip too (or Chip Two).

I'm not sure why we got both Turtles, but I know for sure that what's meant to be… will be.

HOOTERVILLE HEIST

Another trip in the RV. This time we're towing our trailer and headed to southwest Tennessee, to the town of Oblivione.

Oblivione. The name rang a bell. Then, I remembered why. I'd read a short story titled "Ex Oblivione" by H.P. Lovecraft. It's about a dying man who was fed up with life. He took opium to help him sleep. He had a recurring dream about paradise, but he couldn't enter because the gates were locked. He was obsessed with entering paradise, so he took more opium, hoping to return to the dream and pass through the gates. Finally, one night, he found the gates open. What he discovered through those gates wasn't paradise, but desolation and emptiness.

Hopefully, the only similarity with our trip to Oblivione, Tennessee, and Lovecraft's "Oblivione", is the name and not an omen that our coming venture would leave us empty-handed.

NUCKED!

We were on the hunt for an antique car from Idora Park. There were 13 of these cars at Idora, three-fifths the size of a Ford Model "T". Each car had a gas engine and traveled along a fixed course, guided by a single, winding vertical steel plate about six inches tall. The steel plate's job was to keep the cars on course and still allow the driver to steer the car, but only slightly. Steer too far left or right and a mechanism under the car contacted the steel plate and that plate straightened the car, keeping it on course. There was no off-course joy riding.

We found one of these cars on a website called "Arrow Development Cars". There are several styles of "Arrow" cars. Each style is rare and highly sought after by collectors. This particular car wasn't up for sale but was posted on the website. The description stated that it was "from an amusement park in Ohio or Pennsylvania". The car was rough, neglected and abused. But I knew it was from Idora Park and I had to have it. It wasn't for sale, but it was worth a try.

What alerted me to this particular car's significance was a photo on that website showing the car's painted license plate, #105. There was a wear mark and scratch through the #105. The number, wear mark and scratch matched several old photos of the license plate on a light blue colored Idora Park Hooterville Highway car with white spoke wheels. Eureka!

Idora Park received their 13 antique Arrow cars in time for the start of the 1969 season. There's no record indicating where the cars came from before their arrival at Idora Park, whether it was from Arrow Development or if they were purchased from another amusement park. Idora Park's office and most of its contents, including the park records burned to the ground in the fire, April 26, 1984.

When the 13 cars arrived at Idora Park in 1969 the three park owners met to come up with a name for the new ride. They were stumped. Owner Lenny Cavalier went home that evening and described the newly acquired ride to Mary, his wife. He told her that he and his partners couldn't come up with a name. Mary had an idea.

She stayed home all day with their six children and often let them watch the popular television shows, *Petticoat Junction* and *Green Acres*. Both shows were situation comedies, located in the fictional farming community of Hooterville. Mary suggested to Lenny that the park name the new ride Hooterville Highway.

Lenny laughed at the suggestion and told Mary that the other owners "would never go for that name". The next day when Lenny arrived home from work Mary asked if they'd settled on a name for the new ride. Lenny laughed, "Yeah, you were right, we're calling it Hooterville Highway!" And that's truthfully how the ride got its name. Lenny and Mary told me the story at one of our museum openings.

I had no evidence of the whereabouts of the other 12 Idora Park Hooterville cars despite numerous attempts to locate them. Luckily, 1983 photos of the blue car #105 and its scratched license plate at Idora Park matched photos of the car I'd found on the Arrow Owners website. There aren't enough photos of Hooterville cars at Idora Park that would help me pick out distinguishing markings that I could look for when searching other Arrow cars. Thirty-nine years have passed since Idora Park closed its gates forever and no one has come forward who knows the whereabouts of another car. But at least we found one!

We could have taken my truck with the trailer, but let's face it, the RV is fun. Well, it's fun when nothing breaks. Breakage of some component or another should be an expectation for anyone who has an RV. After all, our roads aren't perfect. In fact, most of our roads are pathetic, having potholes, uneven surfaces, debris on the road, stray animals, other drivers, etc… Imagine your house constantly experiencing earthquakes. That's what an RV experiences every time you take it on a trip. And I like scenic back roads. As a result, stuff shakes loose, things break. Still, camping is fun.

NUCKED!

Our RV doesn't get great gas mileage. We'd traveled almost 300 miles and the fuel gauge was leaning toward empty. I needed to stop soon. Luckily, we were approaching an exit. The name of the town was RockPaperScissors, Kentucky. When I saw the name of the town on the exit sign, I knew that we had to stop. Spike agreed. She was with Nuck and me on this trip.

Who the heck names a town RockPaperScissors, and why?

I took the exit and pulled the RV into the McDonald's restaurant parking lot. Spike, Nuck and I walked inside. Right away I noticed something peculiar about the place.

The young girl working behind the counter was breastfeeding a baby. It stunned me! I tried not to look at her breast or her baby. But it was so unexpected that it's hard not to stare. Why is she breastfeeding while working? This was strange to say the least. Now, don't get me wrong, I'm all for breastfeeding, even breastfeeding in public. I mean when a baby is hungry, it needs to eat. It's a natural thing. But this girl was an employee, waiting on customers.

The girl spoke first, "What chall wantin' ta eat?"

NUCK: (wide-eyed, looking at me) Boss, what language that?

ME: (giving him a cold look) Quiet, we're in Kentucky. They talk a little different down here, but I think I understand.

It was difficult to look the girl in the eye without seeing the baby as it nursed. I tilted my head way back, but found my eyes traveling down, from her face to her… well, baby. I wasn't looking at her breast. Honest! It wasn't even exposed, but the whole scene of breastfeeding a baby while serving customers was hard to digest. My head was moving around like Stevie Wonder in an effort not to stare.

ME: I'll have a Big Mac, fries and a coke. My friend here will have a chicken nugget Happy Meal with apple slices and milk. How about you, Spike?

GIRL: (smug look on her face) Ain't got no Happy Meal and ain't no milk 'less ya'll wantin' a glass a what I'm feedin' my little sister here.

SPIKE: (chuckling, looking me in the eye) You know what, I'm going to sit out this little conversation. You order for me. I'm going to have a seat in one of the booths.

I nodded at Spike, then looked back at the girl.

ME: (shocked, gulping) Your sister? That's not really your sister, is it? You're breastfeeding your sister?

GIRL: You ain't from 'round here, eh?

ME: Uh no, we live in Ohio.

GIRL: Where's O-hi-ya?

ME: Where's Ohio? Are you kidding? It's your northern neighbor, one state north! We share a border. How could you not... You know what... never mind. That's not important, but uh, is that really your sister? Never mind that too, I don't think I want to know. So, uh, what do you serve here?

GIRL: (sassy attitude) Mister, we ain't got none a that stuff you ordered. We serve hot dogs, chili, cornbread, sody pop and beer. That's all. This here ain't no fancy-dancy McDonald's restaurant like you city folk get all dressed up for. This is McDavid's. Didntcha notice the double wide arches outside?

ME: What? Double wide arches? You folks are going to get sued by McDonalds when they see that you're copying their look. Never mind. But tell me, is this town really named RockPaperScissors?

GIRL: Why yessir, it truly is.

ME: But that's a kids' game. Who names a town RockPaperScissors?

GIRL: (smiling and pointing) Well, ain't this yer lucky day, Mr. O-hi-ya! The feller what invented that game is eatin' in our restaurant right now. That's him right 'cher!

My eyes followed her pointing finger to a guy sitting by himself at a booth, obviously enjoying his meal because he was licking his fingers. I'd place his age as early 20s, barely. I opened my eyes wide in surprise and turned back to look at the girl. I noticed right away that the baby was gone. Where the heck did the baby go? Oh well, this made it less of a distraction to look her in the eye.

ME: That guy didn't invent Rock-Paper-Scissors. He's maybe 20 years old. Rock-Paper-Scissors has been around since way before that kid was even born.

GIRL: Unh unh mister! Not here in Kentucky!

ME: What? What does that mean, not here in Kentucky? When something is discovered or invented it happens only once – for everywhere, including Kentucky! Rock-Paper-Scissors has been around a long, long time. That kid didn't invent anything. He's just a puppy!

GIRL: (stern look on her face) Mister, I ain't arguin' with you. Are you gonna order or leave?

NUCK: Don't leave! I hungry boss! You say we stop, eat. Chili dog sound good.

ME: (looking at Nuck) Go ahead and order. But no chili! I'll have a hotdog with fries and the same for Spike. There's no way any of us is having unknown chili on this trip, with hours of driving to go.

The girl wrote up the order on a ticket pad. The bill came to $16.95. I pulled out my credit card, then noticed there was no credit card reader on the countertop.

GIRL: (shaking her head and looking at the credit card) No sir, we don't do that here. You pay with cash money, real money, dollar beels!

Sheesh! I reached into my pocket and pulled out the little cash I had on me. It was a $5 bill and a pile of $1 bills. I started counting with the $5, then the ones. I noticed the girl staring intently at the "beels", quietly repeating my count…

Five… five, six… six, seven… seven, eight… eight,

It kinda got a little cute and funny hearing her accent echoing my count. She looked so intent, staring at the bills as I counted… nine… nine, ten… ten, eleven… she stopped counting.

I waited to hear her say "eleven". She didn't. It startled me I guess, so I looked at her. Her mouth was hanging open and she was still staring at the dollar bills. I repeated, "eleven" and looked at her for her response. Nothing. She didn't say "eleven".

ME: (looking at the girl) You stopped counting. Why?

GIRL: Mister, I'm from Kentucky.

I understood immediately. I handed her all my cash, $19 and told her to keep the change.

ME: Nuck, I'll be right back, gotta wash my hands in the restroom.

GIRL: Here, you'll need the key.

She hoisted a cinder block up onto the countertop. There was a chain wrapped through the thing and a key attached to the opposite end of the chain.

ME: Seriously?

GIRL: Don't want no one walkin' off wit the key!

When I returned, I saw that Nuck was sitting in the booth with Spike. I joined him, sitting directly across.

NUCK: (chuckling) Everything come out okay, boss?

ME: Old joke. Real funny, clown. I only washed my hands.

I saw the girl approaching with our tray of food and three "sody pops". She had a lit cigarette hanging off her lip. I was shocked!

ME: (loudly) You're smoking? In here? What the…?

GIRL: (annoyed) Look mister, you ain't in no O-hi-ya no more.

The girl set our food down in front of us and walked away. I heard the baby wail from somewhere on the other side of the food counter.

GIRL: (shouting in the direction of the scream) Awright, awright, I'm comin' ya little monster. I'll be glad when momma gets outta the pokey and takes you home. You is definitely interferin' with my career!

Nuck ignored the girl and was already starting in on his food.

NUCKED!

SPIKE: (smiling about something) Nuck tells me he went to church last week and learned something interesting.

I looked at her, puzzled.

NUCK: (between bites of his hotdog) Yes, boss. I go to church last week. Interesting. You know Jesus have pet?

ME: (glancing at him, then at Spike) Really? I didn't know that. But I've only been to church a handful of times. I'm surprised you went to church. I know that Jesus rode a donkey. What kind of pet did he have, a dog?

NUCK: No dog, boss. Opossum.

ME: (skeptical) What? Get out of here. Jesus had an opossum for a pet? An opossum is no pet. They said that in church?

NUCK: (speaking calmly, matter of fact) Preacher say so, Jesus have 12 opossum! 12!

ME: 12 opossums, eh? You really are a knucklehead. Jesus had 12 APOSTLES not 12 OPOSSUMS! You better find another church or get your hearing checked.

NUCK: I pretty sure preacher right, Jesus have 12 opossum.

ME: No knucklehead, you heard wrong. Jesus had followers that were called apostles, not opossums. Remind me to buy you a Bible and a hearing aid.

Spike just shook her head and laughed, offering me no help whatsoever in explaining to Nuck that he'd heard wrong in church.

Our trip was mostly uneventful after we left McDavid's restaurant in RockPaperScissors. There was a gas station in the town, so I filled up the RV and we set off. But I couldn't help chiding Nuck, every once in a while, about Jesus' pet opossums.

Once we crossed into western Tennessee it was starting to get dark, so we began watching signs for campgrounds. We took the exit for a town called Teefus. Two miles from that exit was a campground named Ocean's Edge. Geography was never my strongest subject, but I was pretty sure there's no ocean edge anywhere in Tennessee.

We'd never been to this campground. Spike did a quick internet search while I drove toward the place. It had all the necessary hookups a camper needs: electrical power, potable water and sewage disposal. The sewage disposal is called the dump site.

Unfortunately, this campground didn't have individual dump sites at the camping spaces, meaning that the black water (toilet water) and grey water (water from the shower and sinks) would have to be dumped at a single dump site that was used by everyone at the campground. Luckily, we had a blue tote. It's a blue plastic, fully enclosed wagon-like thing with wheels that you dump your black and grey tanks into, then pull the blue tote to the dump site and dump its contents. It's somewhat easier than driving over to the dump site in the RV. When a camper has an opportunity to dump tanks, you take it, and you dump tanks. I decided beforehand that I'd be dumping our tanks with the blue tote before leaving the campsite.

We pulled up to the campground and parked at the front gate, which was closed. There's usually an office for checking in at a campsite. This place had no office building. Seeing no one around, no office to approach, I tapped the RV horn lightly a couple of times hoping to get the attention of someone in charge.

A small Asian woman who appeared to be in her late 60s approached us from inside the campground. I stepped out of the RV and walked over to greet her. Nuck joined me. Spike stayed in the RV. As the woman approached, I saw a name tag. Ah, an employee!

The top line of her name tag was her name, "Phan" and under her name, "Philippines". I presumed that Philippines designated her place of birth. The third line read "Manger". Okay, so someone can't spell "Manager". That important second letter "a" in the word "Manager", which distinguishes a person in charge of something at work from a dwelling in which animals live, a "Manger".

I greeted "Manger" Phan with "hello". She replied, but I couldn't understand a word she said. She was really angry. About what, I had no idea. She was practically yelling at me. Her language sounded like a mix of maybe Filipino and Deep South. I was stumped. Nuck talks in broken English, so I looked at him and shrugged my shoulders. Maybe he knew what Phan was saying.

NUCK: (confused) Boss, lady talk backward!

Phan's eyes grew wide! She understood Nuck and by her reaction didn't appreciate his comment. Once again, she launched into a tirade of unintelligible words, all the while pointing at the gate and our RV. I tried again to get her to slow down, and she did, but continued yelling, slowly. It didn't help. We couldn't understand her. I asked her to use the phonetic alphabet to spell out what she was trying to say, you know "A" is Alpha, "B" is Bravo, "C" is Charlie, etcetera…

That didn't help. At least I knew that she understood English. I'm no good at charades so her facial, hand and body gyrations weren't telling me anything other than she was furious about something. Accents have always been difficult for me to decipher. I couldn't tell what language she was using. Then, the light bulb over my head went on and I had an epiphany…

ME: Nuck, go ask Spike to give you that language interpreter thing. It should be in the cabinet over the master bed.

I saw a puzzled look on Phan's face. That quickly turned to obstinance and folded arms. She was not a happy camper, and I had no idea what demons possessed this woman. Maybe the language interpreter would clear things up. Nuck returned with the language device, and I turned it on, pointed the microphone end toward Phan, and asked her to speak. The device is automatic. It will hear the language, process it and convert that language into English. All Phan needed to do was speak her language. And she did, slowly. I smiled and waited for the device to interpret her words.

Nothing.

I checked to make sure the switch was turned on, then checked the battery meter, it read 95% power. The device was on automatic but can be switched to individual languages. I thought maybe the device would respond to her Filipino "twang", but no. And there wasn't a selection that read "Tennessee". Amazingly, I saw a selection on the device labeled "Hillbilly". I was shocked that in this age of rampant political correctness that a device could be constructed with a word that some would consider offensive. "Hillbilly"? I flipped the device over in my hands and saw the words printed on the back, "Made in China". Hmm, it figures.

The language interpreter was still flipped to "Hillbilly" when Phan began speaking. Her voice triggered the device!

PHAN: (scowling, via the interpreter device) Why ya'll honkin' that horn? I was on my way here. Ya'll didn't haf to honk that thing! Now, how long ya'll plan on stayin' here? Ya'll a pain in my neck, all ya'll campin' people! Ya'll got dogs? No dogs! Ya'll pay the fee now an I let you out at 11 in the AM on the day ya'll s'posed to leave. One minute late and ya'll pay another night…

She went on and on. What an angry person. What makes a person so nasty? I nodded to her, paid the fee for one night, climbed into the RV and started driving to the camping space that she assigned to us. On the way inside the gate, I noticed that the campground held quite a few permanent residents. There were campers with insulation skirts around the bottom, a perfect indicator of a semi-permanent or at least long-term resident. Lots of the camper vehicles were old and rundown. There were a few that looked newer, then there were the transients, like us.

Space #29 was on a hill. Most of the open spaces were on flat ground, but I think Phan was punishing us by putting us on a hill. The nose of the RV would be facing downhill, the rear of the RV would be uphill. That imbalance causes problems with dumping the black and grey water tanks even with a blue tote.

We spent an uneventful night, but in the morning, we heard what had to be Phan, yelling unintelligibly about something. I looked out the door and saw her, maybe fifty yards away, arms flailing and yelling at a young woman who appeared to be in her early twenties. I don't think the young girl understood what was being said. I thought about giving her my language interpreter but figured that would likely trigger another Phan tantrum directed at me, so I decided against it. The young girl was on her own.

I was ready to leave grumpy Phan's campground and get back on the road after I dumped our tanks. I pulled out the blue tote and called Nuck to help. This could be tricky. The tote needed to be downhill a ways from the RV in order to empty the tanks. But gravity can be a wonderful thing. The slope of the hill will cause the tote, located downhill to fill quickly. I retrieved the dump hose, connected it to the RV tanks, then had Nuck put the tote in position a couple of yards away, down the hill. The opposite end of the dump hose was stretched out to connect to the tote. All I had to do was pull the handle on the RV's black (toilet water) tank and the contents will flow through the dump hose and into the blue tote. Easy peasy.

Once the tote is full of black water it is brought to the dump site and emptied. The grey water goes into the tote next, then it too gets a trip to the dump site. Grey water is much cleaner than the black tank toilet water. So, once the black water tank is empty the handle is pushed closed, then the grey water tank handle is opened. The grey water passing through the dump hose tends to give the dump hose its first "clean", hopefully removing any black water that remained in the dump hose. The final step is to push clean water through the dump hose to remove any grey water in the hose. Maybe that sounds confusing, but it's really easy - most of the time.

Everything looked good so I pulled the black water tank handle to let the tank drain into the blue tote. The dump hose immediately reacted, filled and stretched a little longer as the toilet water rushed downhill, through the dump hose, toward the blue tote. I watched, making sure everything was going smoothly when I was suddenly distracted by grumpy Phan. I heard her yelling about something. She was at the base of the hill, yelling at that same young lady again. I just shook my head. What is she so angry about? My guess is that she's one of those miserable, unhappy souls who has to be angry all the time and must have drama in her life. Most of us know someone like that. How sad and what a waste of time and waste of life.

I directed my attention back to the dump hose. The RV's toilet contents were slowing down, emptying. Very little of the nasty stuff was flowing now. I closed the black tank handle as the last of the effluent was moving through the hose, toward the tote. That's when something caught my eye. Did the blue tote just move a smidgen, or did I imagine it?

No, it did move, maybe. Yes, it just moved again. The wheels had been cocked sideways, but now they were slowly turning straight, almost pointing downhill. The weight of the black water rushing into the tote made the wheels turn! I felt my face flush red and a feeling of panic rose in my chest. Surely Nuck pushed the wheel locks in place, right? I yelled for him…

ME: (yelling) NUCK! Come here, QUICK!

The tote wheels turned again, a little straighter now and I saw the tote move forward a tad, pulling the dump hose tighter, just a bit.

ME: (nearing panic mode) NUCK! HURRY!

I ran toward the blue tote. I was almost upon it when suddenly, the dump hose, which had been straining to hold the tote in place, let go from its connection at the tote. The tote started rolling downhill, slowly. The remainder of the dump hose contents began spewing from the detached dump hose, a gallon of stinky poopy toilet water all over the grass. Uh oh.

But the real horror was the blue tote. It started to pick up speed thanks to the hill and that wonderful thing called gravity. But gravity was not my friend today. Seeing the blue tote roll answered my question, the wheel locks had not been engaged. I started running. I needed to catch that blue tote, but it had a head start and my days of sprinting were over about thirty years ago. I pushed myself as fast as I could. The tote was faster. I ran after it anyway as it bumped and raced straight ahead down the grassy knoll. A big blue missile full of poop and pee headed for who knows where, with me flailing behind, way behind.

I couldn't catch it, but I ran after it any way. I looked ahead of the tote, calculating, no guessing its intended route, hoping it would come to a flat piece of ground that would slow the thing and eventually stop it. Instead of flat ground there was a small concrete curb maybe eight inches tall, at the very base of the hill. At least it would stop the tote if something else didn't stop it first. I didn't see anything else though that might slow or stop the tote. The darn thing looked like it had a mission. It was probably going to smash right into that curb. And standing on that curb with her back to us was Phan, yelling at that young twenty-something girl. I was mortified! I kept running and praying.

Then I saw it, from the corner of my eye, a flash of something moving rapidly. A small black-clad object farther down the hill, running, much faster than me, across the hill, perpendicular to the blue missile, on an intercept course with the tote. Something amazing, thankfully, was happening right before my eyes! It was Nuck! He was moving like a Patriot missile zeroed in for the intercept kill on a scud missile. He was farther down the hill from me and closing fast on the blue tote, bearing down on the unsuspecting blue poop target from a right angle, moving laterally across the open field. Just one more yard to go and tragedy would be averted. All he needed to do was maintain his current pace and grab the blue tote's handle, change its trajectory, slow it down, then stop it.

But he didn't keep running.

Instead, at the last second, he dove through the air in an effort to catch the tote. Suddenly, as if in a movie, time slowed almost to a standstill. I saw this happen before. It's some kind of ninja trick to dramatize an event. You've seen things like this in Hollywood movies. I don't know how they do it, but everything moves in almost freeze frame slow motion for just an instant or two. I try to understand it somewhat, in terms of a record player with three speeds, 33 revolutions per minute (rpms), 45 rpms and 78 rpms. Life moves normally, at a pace of 45 rpms. Ninjas can slow the world around them down to 33 rpms when performing amazing ninja moves. When they need to hurry things up, they can speed their world up to 78 rpm. Maybe that helps you to better understand what I'm trying to describe and what was happening right before my eyes. Nuck slowed everything around him to 33 rpm while I watched. He was diving midair - in slow motion.

Now, his speed was fine while he was running, but you can't pick up speed if you're diving vertically through the air, even if you can slow everything down to 33 rpm. There's no rocket motor to propel a person through the air, you slow down and lose speed, not gain it. It did look graceful though and it seemed like he'd timed the leap perfectly. Almost.

WHUMP, he was back at 45 rpm when his outstretched body hit the ground hard. One hand was extended out toward the blue tote in a desperate move to grab or nudge some piece of it off course. He missed, by inches. The tote buzzed right by him as he lay on the grass. It looked to be doing 78 rpm. That thing was on a mission. I was afraid to watch but did so any way. There was nothing else that either of us could do now. The tote was maybe 10 yards from the curb and accelerating toward Phan and the girl. Even if I yelled, they'd never react in time. I prayed neither of them would step down from that curb and be struck by the heavily poop-laden blue tote.

I saw the young girl look up and peer over Phan's shoulder. She must have been distracted by Nuck's flying act. She saw the blue tote heading toward them. Her face contorted, her eyes opened wide and she pointed at the speeding tote, but Phan didn't flinch. Phan's back was to the runaway tote. She was intent on yelling at the girl even as the girl turned and ran away, fast. Phan threw her hands up in the air in frustration as the girl took off. I imagined Phan must be thinking to herself, that this girl just runs off in the middle of a scolding…

Phan had her back to us, but I could tell that she sensed something was about to happen. She dropped her arms to her side, turned her head, cocking it to one side as her ears picked up some strange, unfamiliar sound that she couldn't quite identify. I could almost read the thought bubble above her head, even in that strange dialect of hers, "What is that rumbling sound that I hear?"

If she would just turn around, she'd find out what the approaching noise was and just maybe she could run away before the tote slams into that curb she's standing on! I was watching the preview of a train wreck and couldn't pull my eyes away. I was praying that she'd run away or that the tote wouldn't hit a bump and jump the curb, hitting her. Finally, but too late, Phan turned her head and then her body toward the approaching sound. She probably caught only a glimpse of something headed her way before the blue torpedo impacted the curb. I saw her mouth open wide and her arms flew up in front of her face. Too late. Oh, the humanity!

It sounded like an explosion. KA-BA-BLAM!

The blue tote impacted the curb at great speed. The curb withstood the blow, but the blue tote did not. It collapsed like an accordion. The front of the tote nose-dived while the rear section came up off the ground a few inches. I was petrified that the tote might climb the curb and hit Phan. Thankfully, that didn't happen. What did happen was maybe worse. The tote split wide open after turning into an accordion, propelling its disgusting contents up into the air toward Phan. The stuff hung in the air for barely an instant, but what goes up must come down. Gravity works that way.

I guess you could say that the s#!* hit the Phan, literally! She wasn't hurt, but she was covered in stinky brown stuff from head to toe. She was shocked, confused and horrified, her arms flailing as if she were drowning. She was spitting up muck, screaming and then went to her knees, vomiting. I didn't need the interpreter device to understand the meaning. I wondered if this incident might teach her to control her mouth and temper, but I had my doubts.

I looked at Nuck and he looked at me. I saw a smile cross his lips. I stifled a laugh. This wasn't funny. Okay, so maybe it was. But we knew without speaking that we had to get the heck out of there, fast. We took off running for the RV. I left the dump hose laying on the ground, a gift for Phan. Spike had been watching the tote fiasco from inside the RV. When she saw Nuck and me run to the RV she strapped herself into her seat and was ready to skeedaddle. I fired up the RV and we made it out the gate and turned left, heading for Oblivione, Tennessee, and the Hooterville Highway car from Idora Park. I was glad to put Phan in our rear-view mirror. I made a mental note to buy a replacement blue tote when we get home.

We made it to the tiny town of Oblivione and found the Hooterville Highway car's owner by asking questions at the local post office. Post office folks in small towns see and know everything about their town. They made a phone call to the man, and I was able to speak to him. He said he'd consider selling and invited Spike, Nuck and me over to see the car.

No, I didn't tell the fella that I knew the car's history. Doing that nearly backfired on me more than once and I learned my lesson. I'd bought an Idora Park game machine from a guy and he helped me load it into my truck. After the game was loaded, I closed the truck's tailgate and the guy was able to see my truck's vanity tag, "IDORA". He looked at me and asked if I was the guy who collects Idora Park stuff. His mood changed when I said yes. He replied, "If I'd known that I'd have charged you more!"

No kidding! Nice guy, eh?

So, if the owner of this Hooterville Highway car finds out that I know the car's history at Idora Park and that we collect artifacts from Idora Park he might think he's got a sucker on the line. I didn't want to pay more than necessary to get the car.

We looked over the car. It was rough, abused by way of neglect. It had sat outside for decades, unprotected from the weather. The man said he'd bought the car in Florida. All he knew was that the previous owner, a woman, was possibly from Ohio but he knew nothing about the car. He liked the look of the car, so he bought it and planned its restoration, but never got around to it. He lost interest within a year or two and the car went outside.

I feigned lack of interest in the car because of its deteriorated condition. But I really wanted it badly. I just couldn't let the owner know that. We could fix this damage. We could get the car rebuilt, maybe even restored. I touched every rotted piece of wood, cracked fiberglass body panel, rusted and broken frame rail, the rotted tires and the shredded roof material, not mentioning the damage out loud, yet making sure that the owner saw me touch those damaged areas. It's a nonverbal tool that I find helpful in price negotiation. Calling out the flaws can put the owner in a defensive mood. I was letting him know that I saw the flaws without saying so. I did tell him that I'd give the car a good home if he was willing to part with it.

It worked. We made a fair deal, shook hands and Nuck and I loaded the Hooterville car onto our trailer. We headed home, bypassing Phan's campground and made it safely home in two days.

Within a year the restoration process was started and six months later the car was restored, a joint effort by Spike, me and the instructors and students from Mr. Joe Sander's Auto Collision Repair Class and Mr. Joe Merritt's Diesel Engine Repair Class at MCCTC. The Idora Park Hooterville Highway car, license plate #105 now looks and runs better than new.

Hootie on the first day of school at MCCTC with some of the Auto Collision Repair Class students

SPIKE'S SIDE OF THE STORY

Wow, where do I start with this one? Let's see… we've had more than our fair share of meals in tiny little towns where former fast-food restaurants are now a backwoods diner with odd things on the menu.

Most of the time those places are amazing, the people friendly and the food fabulous. Certainly, much better than the run of the mill fast food that was once served in the same building.

But every once in a while, we get a situation that makes us wonder if the people around us have ever stepped foot outside of their tiny little town, or for that matter, ever will. We usually walk away counting our blessings and saying a quick prayer for all that we have experienced in our lives.

And I'm here to tell you that language barriers can be very real not just when you travel to places unknown but sometimes worse when it's known.

NUCKED!

We've found ourselves many times in conversations with people that, no matter how hard we try to understand them, we just can't.

One such time, Jim literally said "Spell it phonetically". When that didn't work, he told the person, "Listen, I don't know if you just asked me for a slice of pizza or directions to the bathroom". The gentleman laughed, slowed the cadence of his speech and explained the nature of his accent. English was his native tongue, but his regional accent is legend for being incomprehensible.

We laugh about it now, but when it was happening, we both wanted to smack him.

And the blue tote story… well our experience wasn't quite so dramatic or funny but indeed we did have a blue tote break loose, get free and make a bit of a stinky yucky mess…

That's kind of how we felt during our misadventure getting the Hooterville car (we lovingly call it "Hootie" now). This is a long sordid story that includes having Hootie's seller behave less than honorably in other dealings with us (that's putting it nicely). The seller had $2,500 of money we'd paid him for items that he never delivered… nor did he return our money.

Right about now you're asking why we would ever do business with him again… Good question. I wouldn't have. But I'm not Mr. Idora. Jim wanted Hootie. And all these years later, I'm glad that he did and that he was so persistent in his mission.

The deal for Hootie was made several years before we were allowed to take possession of it… and before we'd had our less than honorable dealing with this guy.

As time went by Jim kept his relationship with this guy as good as he could. The whole time he had me in his ear asking him when we were going to get our $2,500 back.

Jim would tell me, "I don't know, but we'll get it".

Eight years…

That's how long it took to get it back. Well sort of.

When it came time to finally execute on the agreement for the Hootie car the seller balked. He changed the agreed upon price of $2,500 to $5,000. We both knew he was just trying to find a way to write off the $2,500 he owed us and still get $2,500 for Hootie.

Jim negotiated with him and eventually agreed to write off his debt and give him an additional $1,000. The seller agreed, the deal was done, and Jim loaded Hootie onto our trailer and brought it home.

Hootie was in horrible condition and took lots of time, skill and money to restore. But as Jim says, it now looks and runs better than new.

And what of the seller? He came back to us after Hootie was restored and demanded that we place a plaque on it saying it was from his collection. We refused. We bought and paid for it. We restored it. We don't put plaques on things we purchase.

After hours of begging and pleading, Jim compromised with the seller and told him he'd put a plaque on it… on the underside of the floor where no one can see it.

The s#!* hit the Phan.

Kyle Amey giving Hootie a thumbs up

LIFE LESSON: Live on your own terms

The deal for Hootie took eight years to complete and cost about 30% more than our original agreement, but Jim got it done.

Now, you might say, "but not on your terms". I disagree. We always knew the deal Jim made in the beginning wouldn't be the final deal. We had seen enough of the seller's dealings to know that he wouldn't stand by his word. But Jim knew that eventually, with time, patience and negotiation, he'd get the deal he wanted.

I, on the other hand, spent eight years harping on Jim that I thought this guy's lack of integrity and narcissism would prevent him from making and keeping any fair deal Jim might want, and that we'd never see our $2,500 again.

We were both right.

We didn't get the deal that was originally set. We didn't get our $2,500 back. But we did get the Hooterville car and that, above all else, was what we wanted.

There will never be a plaque that says it's from the collection of…

SWAMP HONEY

Nuck and I were headed to Louisiana to look at a piece of lost history, the two Soldiers that guarded Idora Park's Kiddieland. Somehow, they ended up down south.

The Soldiers are nearly 12 feet tall. They are actually Nutcrackers, I think, but look a lot like the beefeater guards in England. And maybe that's what they actually are, beefeaters. I just don't know. So, I'm just going to call them Soldiers. There's not much history on them, but we know they arrived at Idora Park in 1951 when Kiddieland took the place of the swimming pool. But where the Nutcrackers originally came from and where they went immediately after Idora Park closed is a mystery. We do know that they somehow ended up in Louisiana in a little parish called Wakapeapea, pronounced "Whack-a-pea-pea". An old Cajun name?

NUCKED!

How did we find the Soldiers? How else? Nuck does this for a living, finding Idora Park artifacts wherever they may be hidden. We find the artifact, then contact the current owner or the person who knows the artifact's whereabouts. Then, we travel to the artifact's location and attempt to work out a deal with the owner. We aren't always successful. Some people just aren't interested in parting with their treasure and sometimes people are mistaken, and the item isn't from Idora. If you read our book "NUCKED!" You know exactly what I mean.

Nuck wasn't excited about a trip to Louisiana. He'd heard too many stories about spirits, ghosts, goblins, werewolves and monsters. Louisiana has one heck of a history with the "undead". Nuck gets spooked by certain states where unexplained supernatural things occur. You know, like the Mothman in West Virginia and Bigfoot or Sasquatch in Northern California. Then there's the extraterrestrial aliens in Roswell New Mexico, the Jersey Devil in New Jersey, Pigman in Angola, New York, the Youngstown Yeti, the Green Man of Beaver Falls Pennsylvania, and so on.

Okay, so maybe I made up the Youngstown Yeti, but the others are supposedly based on actual sightings. And there really was a Green Man in Pennsylvania. He was injured in 1918 by an electrical line at age eight while climbing a pole that carried live trolley electric power. The injury disfigured his face. He lost his eyes, nose and right arm. The accident also gave a green tint to his skin. In the mid 1970s I went on several missions with friends to find the Green Man, but never did see him. Many others did though. Look him up! Just do an internet search for "Green Man Pennsylvania". He was real. The Green Man died in 1985, aged 74.

According to Nuck, Wakapeapea is on the bayou, a strip of land shaped like a finger that juts out into of all things, a swamp. It's a tiny Cajun Indian reservation with a history of werewolf sightings, supposedly. Yep, werewolves. I promised Nuck that we wouldn't be there during a full moon. As for me, when I hear the word Louisiana or bayou I think of mosquitoes, swamps, snakes and alligators. Maybe piranha too, but I'm not sure about those. I'm not concerned about werewolves. Alligators however, those scare me. Swamps scare me too. You never know what lives in them, things that can get you. Swamp things.

Once, back in the mid 1990s, Spike and I were driving somewhere way down south near a Florida swamp, and we saw something big and dead on the side of the road. She wrote about it in the chapter, "Dead Things on a Train". The thing was jet black in color and huge, the biggest dead creature I'd ever seen, and I was curious to know what it was. Maybe a black bear? I made a U-turn at the earliest opportunity, then another U-turn onto the dead thing's road and drove back to get a closer look. I pulled the car up close to the thing, got out of the car and the gassy odor of swamp hit my nostrils.

I walked up to the creature and immediately could tell what it was by its huge black head and the fangs jutting from its open mouth, a dead jaguar! Its paws were huge and had big sharp claws! Scared the heck out of me! I started imagining all kinds of scary thoughts. What if someone's car broke down out here and they had to change a tire or walk for gasoline? This place has jaguars! Then it occurred to me, if there's one jaguar out here, there's probably more of them and here I am standing out in the open: jaguar bait! The hair on my neck stood up and I ran back to the car, jumped in and took off, fast. True story! I still get the heebie jeebies when I think of that day. I won't get out of a vehicle anywhere near a swamp. And yet, that's exactly where Nuck and I were going, for a greater cause – Idora Park history.

Nuck watched the weather and checked the calendar closely and picked an overcast period of three days with practically no moon showing in Wakapeapea, hopefully plenty of time to get the two Kiddieland Soldiers without being ripped apart by werewolves.

I told Nuck to pack enough clothing and personal items for a four-day trip. He doesn't have much of a wardrobe since he only wears ninja clothes. On the day we were to leave for Wakapeapea Nuck showed up carrying a small black backpack. Something just wasn't right though. A strange, yet familiar odor was coming from Nuck's vicinity. I couldn't quite place the smell, but it was strong.

ME: (nose scrunched) Is that you that stinks? Did you shower this morning? You smell like a moose's armpit!

NUCK: I shower. No stink!

ME: (correcting him) YES, STINK! What's that smell, then? You can't smell that?

Nuck set his backpack on the ground as I moved closer to him. I sniffed him. He stunk like that smell, but the odor wasn't quite as strong as it was a moment earlier. I had an idea.

ME: Open your backpack. Whatever stinks is in your pack! What is it, some Ninja stinky snack? Let me see!

NUCK: Boss, werewolf protection. That all!

ME: What? What kind of protection? That's not pepper spray, is it? Whatever it is, it must have leaked and everything in that pack is going to smell like that! You've got to get rid of whatever stinks and burn that pack and everything in it!

NUCK: (slightly defiant) Boss, I tell you, we need protection!

ME: (pointing at the backpack) Let me see what's in there.

Nuck dejectedly opened the pack, and a waft of the stink was released to the air. I kept my distance. The familiarity of the scent was now pretty obvious. I'd smelled something distinctly similar many times in Italian cooking, but never quite this strong. Nuck reached in and pulled it out, a necklace of onion bulbs!

ME: (surprised, shaking my head) Onions? An onion necklace? You couldn't double or triple bag it in resealable bags to block the smell, you had to stink up everything and ruin your clothes and the backpack? How do you plan on cleaning this stuff now? And, why onions? Garlic is for warding off vampires, but why onions? For werewolves? There's no such thing as werewolves, or vampires either! What else is in there, a silver cross, maybe a wooden stake and mallet? Maybe doggie biscuits?

NUCK: (sheepishly, head hung low) No cross, no stake, no biscuit. I protect you, boss. You old now. Werewolf fast, you slow. Maybe onion help.

ME: (wincing at "old" and "slow") You better watch it! That ice you're skating is thin. I might be "getting" older and slower, but I can still hold my own with anyone. And I don't need protection from a make-believe creature no matter what it is, a werewolf, vampire, Big Foot or unicorns.

NUCK: (offering his expertise) Unicorn gone, boss. They not show up for Ark, miss boat.

I just shook my head at his last comment and thought it better than to say anything. What good does it do me to argue mythical creatures with a three-foot ninja?

NUCK: Three feet AND three-inch, boss!

ME: (puzzled) Hunh? I didn't say anything.

NUCK: (knowingly, one finger tapping his head) I know what you think, boss!

And that had me worried.

But wait, I'm getting ahead of myself. You should know how Nuck found these two Idora Park Kiddieland Soldiers. Well, as is often the case, it starts out with receiving a phone call. Someone happened to see our Facebook page and noticed the Kiddieland Soldiers on one of the photos. The guy called Nuck and said that he's pretty sure that the Soldiers are in Louisiana at a boarded-up cigar store. A native Indian fella owns the cigar store building, and the two Soldiers once stood at either side of the front door. The cigar store owner has since retired, and the building is run down and scheduled for demolition.

NUCKED!

To verify this Nuck had the caller, named Bumpy send us a photo of the Soldiers. Sure enough, they looked like Idora's guys, but they had been re-painted to look like native Indians. The big Nutcracker or beefeater hats were painted to look like Indian headdresses, feathers and all. The faces had warpaint, the chests were bare and painted a pinkish-red color. From the waist down they were painted with tan and brown deerskin-looking pants with painted on fringe. The big block feet were now sandals. I'm surprised that Bumpy was able to tell that these two Indian figures were once Nutcrackers. Or beefeaters.

We got the name of the town from Bumpy, it's the aforementioned little Indian reservation called Wakapeapea and we made our plan to head there. Unfortunately, Bumpy had no contact info for the cigar store owner, other than the location of the store and the store owner's name, which was Squatting Platypus.

Yes, an unusual name, but I've heard many unusual names in my life travels. I even met a fella once from India. His name was Mahatma Kote which sounds like "my hat, my coat". Nothing really surprises me anymore. There are many cultures and names unfamiliar to me in America alone. Squatting Platypus was just another name. I did wonder though, how he got his name. A platypus by design is awfully low to the ground already. How can you tell if one is squatting?

I looked up the name "Squatting Platypus" on the internet. Maybe I could find a photo, an address or phone number or maybe on social media, something that might help me locate Mr. Platypus directly. I had no luck. The "Squatting Platypus" internet search only turned up videos of people walking around like sumo wrestlers. It turns out that walking like that is a great exercise for strengthening one's butt and thigh muscles. This looked like another trip down a blind alley.

But nothing ventured nothing gained, so Nuck and I left for Wakapeapea, Louisiana, a 17-hour drive, on a Wednesday morning. I planned to drive no more than six to eight hours a day and arrive on

Friday. I should have paid closer attention to the date. I didn't realize, until we arrived in Wakapeapea, that Friday fell on the 13th of the month. Friday the 13th of any month is not a good time to be near a Louisiana swamp. But that is when and where we eventually ended up there.

Once we reached Louisiana I continued driving south. We left the main highway and followed the directions to Squaline Road, a narrow blacktop road that ran south by southeast. We stayed on that for eighteen miles, then made a right turn down Reveiw Road, a bumpy gravel road. Nuck noticed the spelling of "Reveiw" and asked me what happened to the English rule "i" before "e", except after "c", usually. I had no answer for him. I just shrugged my shoulders. I think he caught the drift, which was, "It's my first time here too, how the heck would I know?"

We drove another twenty miles hearing the gravel smack up under the truck, then turned left down a dirt road named "Pine Holler". Our destination should only be about another couple of hundred yards once we were on Pine Holler and sure enough, we saw the outline of some old wooden buildings ahead of us.

As we got closer to the buildings, I noticed how run down they were, just beat up old shacks. I'd had a vision in my mind of an old shopping center, but this place was nothing like I'd imagined. It was just a row of different sized dilapidated old lean-tos, broken down shacks and a few rusted out steel shipping containers with the doors missing. The shipping containers were like you'd see on giant merchant ships crossing the oceans. The place looked like an abandoned flea market, not a shopping center.

I pulled the truck up next to the first shack we came to. I cautioned Nuck not to get out of the truck just yet. Who knows what might be lurking out here. There were no signs of human life, but I had no idea what animals might be about. I could smell the gassy odor of the nearby swamp and it reminded me of the huge dead jaguar from years earlier.

NUCK: You think about jaguar, boss?

ME: (nodding my head) Yep. And other things. Smell that swamp? There's other stuff too, like alligators and snakes!

NUCK: Werewolf too, maybe!

ME: (trying not to smirk) Yeah, might be!

NUCK: Really, boss? You tell me no such thing.

ME: And I meant it. There's no such thing as werewolves. Now, let's take a look around and see if we can find Mr. Platypus and those Kiddieland Soldiers.

We got out of the truck, looking around to make sure no biting critters were waiting on the ground. Seeing none, we walked toward one of the buildings, hoping that maybe someone was inside who could point us in the direction of the Kiddieland Soldiers. The building turned out to be boarded up, so we ended up going door to door, shack to shack, always keeping a watchful eye out for creepy crawly things that bite. We found no one. The place was devoid of human life.

NUCK: (head tilted as if listening) Boss! Hear? Music!

ME: (puzzled) What? I don't hear anything except the tinnitus ringing in my ears. I don't even hear any birds, but you hear music?

NUCK: (pointing toward the swamp) Music over there, you hear?

ME: No, I can't hear it, and no, we're not going into the swamp. Strangers don't usually come out of swamps because of what lives in swamps and guess what? We're strangers here! Nope, no swamp.

NUCK: We get close, yell to people and they come out of swamp.

ME: Okay, but I'm not going into the swamp, and neither are you.

We walked in the direction of Nuck's music and sure enough, I heard it too. Music. But, as soon as I realized what kind of music I stopped abruptly and held out my arm to stop Nuck. Crap! Banjos!

ME: I hear it now, Nuck! Those are banjos! That is not a good sign! I think we need to get back to the truck now. Otherwise, we could be walking into a scene from "Deliverance".

NUCK: (smirking) You watch too much movie, boss. Anyway, I protect you. Nobody Deliver you.

ME: Look, the clues that we should get the heck out of here are pretty obvious. A swamp with deadly creatures, rundown shacks and the sound of Cajuns playing banjos tell me that we should hightail it out of here. My gut tells me that it's not a good idea to keep walking that way, but then my brain tells me that there's no one else around here to ask about the Soldiers. I really want to find those Soldiers, but we need to be cautious. Maybe we should have brought a gun, in case we ran into a giant snake or a hungry alligator?

NUCK: (chuckling and holding up his two little hands for me to see) Gun show right here, boss! Ninja hand are weapon! Better than gun!

ME: Those little baby-sized hands, eh? Look, put your little pop guns away and let's just be careful and find out where the banjo player is.

We started walking toward the sound of banjo, turned the corner around a rusted shipping container and saw a swamp. Actually, we smelled it first, swamp gas. The sulfur stink of dead water, dead plants, probably decaying creatures too. But it was the living stuff in the swamp that had me concerned. I looked at Nuck. He had the onion necklace around his neck. I rolled my eyes, said nothing about the onions. You never know, maybe he's on to something.

We saw the banjo player perched on the top stair of the porch of a shack that sat on a chunk of ground surrounded on three sides by swamp water. The banjo player, a young white male wasn't alone. He was accompanied by two other musicians, a harmonica playing young fella with dark tanned skin and an older black man of about fifty with an old washboard. They stopped playing their instruments as we approached the shack. I noticed an old grey dog laying on the porch. It wasn't moving and I wondered if it was alive or how it could have gotten as old as it appeared out here in a swamp with alligators and snakes always looking for a meal. The dog looked stringy. Maybe snakes and alligators were picky eaters?

The washboard player stood up to greet us, descending the porch steps. He stuck out his left hand to shake hands with me and said his name was Specky. I hesitated for just a second because I wasn't expecting to shake left-handed. Then I noticed that Specky had no right arm.

SPECKY: (chuckling) Yep, missing 'Ol Righty, all righty! Gator done took it off when I was still a kid. It's prolly still somewhere out there in that gator's gut. Not sure if a gator belly can digest a human arm bone. He took the whole durn thing, but I took one a his eyes during the tussle, yes I did. Gouged it right out with my left thumb. Broke the thumb doing it, but I got that eye! We still catch sight of him even after all these years. Maybe he's lookin' for his lost eye. Maybe he's lookin' to trade an arm bone for that eye. Anyway, I named that gator Cap'n Jack. Cap'n One-eyed Jack! Oh hey, I like yer onion necklace! Werewolfs hate onions!

I saw Nuck flinch at the mention of "werewolfs". I wanted to correct Specky by telling him that the plural of werewolf is werewolves, not werewolfs, but I got the impression that maybe a class on proper English would be counterproductive just then.

NUCK: (trying to ignore the werewolf subject) Where eye now?

SPECKY: (chuckling again and pointing at the shack) Got it in a jar. When I crawled out of that swamp shy one arm all I wanted was to get patched up 'afore I bled out. I dropped that gator eye on the way to the clinic. Ma found it and stuck it in the only thing close at hand, a bottle of swamp honey.

NUCK: Swamp honey?

SPECKY: Yep, swamp honey. Local drink. A jigger of swamp water and honey harvested from the swamp wasp. You Yankees would call it moonshine. But it's a special kind of moonshine. Gots a real sting to it.

ME: (disbelieving) Wasp honey? You're kidding, right? Wasps don't make honey. Are you sure those aren't bees?

SPECKY: Oh, they wasps all righty. But heck, I'm being rude. Let me introduce you to my friends.

Specky pointed out the banjo player and introduced him as Red. The harmonica guy was Cross-eyed Willy, and the dog was Bumper. We introduced ourselves too.

NUCK: Bumper not move. He okay?

RED: (laughing) Yeah, he good. He jus' ol'. Bumper kinda blind in one eye and cain't see out the other. And kinda deaf too. He cain't smell too good anymore either. Use to be a prize trackin' dog for the county jail, but retired years back. He still get around though and still a pretty good watchdog once in a while.

Maybe Bumper heard his name somehow or his remaining sense of smell caught wind of us, but he stood up and started turning his big head from side to side like a dog does when it's puzzled by a sight or sound. He let out a bark, then ambled over to a wood post on the porch, put his head against the post and started this slow, deep bark. I just watched. I didn't know what the dog was doing.

NUCK: Why he do that?

SPECKY: (laughing) Jus' doing his job the bes' he can, poor ol' boy. He know'd someone's here and probly thinks that wood post is your leg. He cain't see you or hear you too good, but he know strangers is here and he got a watchdog job to do. It takes him a while to get started up though.

I watched the poor thing, standing there with its head against the wood post and barking, thinking it was warning off some uninvited stranger. He'd press his head against the post and push, then back up a step and come forward again with his head against the post, barking slowly the whole time. He kept repeating the bumping back and forth. It reminded me of bumper cars at an amusement park, but with barking. It occurred to me that this poor old dog's name was fitting, "Bumper".

The other guy, Willy, the harmonica player spoke up.

CROSS-EYED WILLY: Bumper is Bumpy's dog. Bumpy called you right, about the cigar store Injuns? He should be along here soon, then ya'll can see them Injuns. Us three cain't go or we'd help. We got a big gig tonight that we needs to practice for.

A gig? A musical gig? These guys play a banjo, a harmonica and a washboard. I couldn't imagine them playing at a venue with live people listening. Maybe Bumpy contributed some important piece of musical instrument that warranted an audience? The drums? Guitar? Oboe? Meanwhile, Bumper continued to bump and bark against that pole. Poor thing.

ME: So, Bumpy's on his way? Does he need to practice with you too?

All three of the fellas started to laugh. Nuck and I looked at each other.

SPECKY: (still laughing) Oh heck no, the only musical instrument Bumpy can play is the radio! And that's only when theys enough gas to run the generator so's we can have 'lectric! But hey, Bumpy should be back soon. You guys can wait here if you like and listen to a few tunes, or wander 'round and do some explorin'. Don't go too deep into the swamp though. They's gators, snakes and other mean critters in there.

NUCK: Werewolf?

SPECKY: (looking skyward, finger to his chin) Cain't says I ever seen or heard a no werewolf in the swamp, but you never know. Some people goes in and never comes out. So's since they don't come out they cain't tell us what they seen or what got 'em.

That was more than enough for me, no swamp tour.

Nuck and I decided to head back the way we came and wait for Bumpy to show up. It didn't take long, maybe ten minutes before we heard a vehicle coming around the dilapidated buildings that we'd walked past earlier. A beat-up old Ford Pinto rolled up beside us and stopped. The driver hopped out, but the Pinto's engine started coughing, spitting and shuddering.

BUMPY: She's a classic, ain't she? Don't like to be shut off though, wants to keep runnin' even after I turn off the key.

ME: That horse is dying. Have you thought about shooting it?

BUMPY: (laughing) She's my baby, jus' needs a little tune-up, that's all. How 'bout we go see them injuns now?

ME: Yeah, we walked around the buildings here, but didn't see them or a cigar store. Are we in the right place?

BUMPY: Yep, we's close. We gotta walk through a short section of swamp to git there.

That didn't make me happy, and I know Nuck wasn't too thrilled either. But we had to do what we came all this way to do, find a piece of Idora Park history and hopefully bring it home.

ME: We can walk? We don't have to go into the water, right? No boat? There's solid ground to walk on and no alligators, snakes, jaguars or other wild things, right?

NUCK: Werewolf?

BUMPY: Nah, no werewolfs, no boat ride through water, and the path is solid ground. I cain't say they won't be a gator or snake along the trail, but they won't bother you if you leave 'em alone.

ME: (skeptical) Sorry, no offense, but I don't believe that. A hungry or angry animal is going to attack no matter how much you ignore them.

BUMPY: (nodding) Probly right! We jus' need to keep our eyes and ears open. Keep our head on a swivel, you know.

I do know! My head is always on a swivel, always looking out for danger.

Bumpy pointed the way and took us right past the house that Nuck and I had just left, minutes earlier. As I'd guessed, Bumpy lived there too. Red, Cross-eyed Willy and Specky were still on the porch playing their instruments. I'd like to say they sounded good, but I don't like to lie. Bumper the dog was there too, still bumping his head against that post.

Bumpy exchanged waves and smiles with his friends and we kept walking southeast into the swamp. Bumpy said it was only a couple hundred yards away. My suspicious mind was working overtime. I wished I'd brought a weapon along. What if we weren't supposed to leave the swamp? Did this guy have a plan to jump us, steal our money and kill us? We didn't know him. I kept scanning for trouble from all around, whether it came on two legs, four legs, or slithered on its belly. Then I saw danger!

Cap'n Jack, the one-eyed alligator was laying across the path and started moving toward us, quickly! He meant business. He had a left eye, no right eye.

BUMPY: (hands outstretched to warn us) Don't move, stand still! A gator won't attack if you stand still!

Nuck and I looked at each other and nodded. We stood still. Bumpy however, took off in a flash, ran right off the path and through the swamp, splashing dark dirty brackish water the whole way.

I immediately thought, now that's a brave guy! He ran so the alligator would go after him. That's why he told us to stay still. But the alligator didn't get that memo. He turned toward us and RAN right at us! I wasn't expecting that, and neither was Nuck.

NUCK: CAP'N JACK, BOSS! RUN!

ME: YOU THINK? GO!

We took off, Nuck sloshing through the swamp, me right behind him and Cap'n Jack on my tail and closing. I'd heard that it's best to run zigzag if chased by an alligator. Gators, according to my internet research, can't zigzag. That's a lie. They can zigzag like a Heisman running back and this one was gaining on me. I broke off from my zigzagging and ran straight ahead, praying that neither Nuck nor I would trip on some hidden tree root under the swamp water.

If Nuck fell I was probably going to fall right over him, and Cap'n Jack would have his choice on the menu, chicken or chicken. Luckily, that didn't happen. We kept running, sloshing through the swamp, high stepping, headed for land. I took a chance, looking over my shoulder for the alligator. Cap'n Jack was there, farther back now. We'd put some distance between him and us, but I wasn't ready to breathe a sigh of relief. Maybe he was done chasing us, decided we weren't worth the effort.

Nuck and I reached dry ground. We looked around to make sure there were no other man-eating critters nearby and we sat down to catch our breath. We each kept one eye on Cap'n Jack. No pun intended. He was about 25 yards away, chomping on something.

NUCK: He like onion, boss!

ME: Hunh? What?

NUCK: I toss onion. Jack catch it.

ME: Nuck, you threw your onion necklace to that alligator, hoping he'd stop and eat the onions? Wow, great thinking. I'm thrilled that it worked because I was just about out of steam. Look at him chomp away! I guess alligators eat onions. Can you believe that jerk Bumpy? We should go find him and give him to Cap'n Jack for dessert. He lied to us. He knew that all he had to do was outrun us and that alligator would go after the slowest bait, you or me. Probably me.

We started walking in the direction that Bumpy ran. The path seemed to be going away from the swamp, I hoped. Sure enough, the path widened into dry ground and more wooden shacks, but these were larger than the first shacks we'd seen, and they didn't appear to have been abandoned for too long. No people were in sight, so we just kept walking along the dirt road near the row of shacks.

The shacks were situated like one continuously long wooden building, as if they were a precursor to the 1960s era strip malls that I remember from my childhood. Only these were wooden and much older. They sort of resembled something from an old spaghetti western movie, but there were no alleyways between buildings.

Some of the stores had signs over the door or on the awnings. Signs that read "AUTO PARTS", "GENERAL STORE", "DRUG STORE", "BAIT & TACKLE", "HARDWARE", "APPLIANCES", "DELI", etc… I expected to see a "SALOON" sign over swinging doors, but no.

I heard some commotion up ahead and put out my hand to slow Nuck. Maybe it was that jerk Bumpy. We crept cautiously along and saw a store that was actually occupied. Humans! The sign out front read "HUNTING BLIND". Oh, okay. I know what those are. I can see the need for hunting blinds. Hunting is big down south and hunting blinds do exactly what the name implies, they are camouflage buildings, huts, or tarps that hide hunters from whatever it is they are hunting, birds, deer, werewolves, unicorns, etc… Someone was inside the store, so we climbed the steps and went inside. There was a lady sitting behind a desk, but no one else in the store and I saw no merchandise for sale. Maybe they only did mail order? I said hello to her.

LADY: Hello there, are you intrested in signing up? If ya are yer a tad late. We're closin' up shop jus' like everone else in these parts. We don' get enough bisness to keep operatin'.

ME: I'm sorry to hear that. But no, I'm no hunter anyway. Is it your location way out here? I'd have guessed that you'd have plenty of hunters out here looking for hunting blinds.

LADY: (laughing) Hunny, you crack me up. You see any huntin' blinds in this store? This store is called "HUNTING BLIND", not "HUNTING BLINDS". We do huntin' tours for the sightless, people who cain't see, blind hunters who jus' wanna shoot somethin'.

I gulped. Blind hunters? Shoot something? How the…?

ME: (in shock) You take blind people on hunting trips? With guns? Is that safe?

LADY: In theory it seemed like it was a market we kin corner. Don't nobody else down here do it. In reality, it weren't such a great idea, 'specially out on the live machine gun range. It is funny though; them blind people practically break dancin' while tryin' to control a Uzi or AK-47 on full auto! Funniest dang thing…

I was horrified. I had to get away. This lady was nuts! What's so funny about that? I needed to get us out of there.

ME: (stammering) Oh hey, look at the time. We're late, gotta run.

Nuck and I took off. I could hear the lady as we headed out the door, she yelled something about stopping by their shooting range should I ever go blind. Nuck and I just looked at each other and shook our heads.

ME: Come on, what a nut. I sure hope we don't meet any more whackos like Bumpy and that lady.

I was about ready to go home. But we walked on. As we approached the end of the row of shops I saw a sign on a store ahead of us, "SMOKE SHOP"! Nuck saw it at the same time.

NUCK: (excited) Boss, this it!

ME: Could be, but I don't see the Nutcracker Soldiers or the Indians. Maybe we can see them through the windows.

We ran up the three steps and onto the porch. The store looked much the same as most of the other stores in the row, kind of like the faded wood buildings in an old west movie. We wiped dirt off a window and peeked through the glass.

NUCK: Man in there, boss. He sit on bench and smoke.

ME: I see him! I wonder if he's the owner, Squatting Octopus?

NUCK: (correcting me) Wrong "pus", boss. Platypus, not Octopus. Knock on window?

ME: Let's try the door. Maybe he's open for business.

We walked to the door, turned the knob and pushed, but the door didn't open. However, the smoking man saw or heard us and turned his head our way.

NUCKED!

ME: Nuck, the door is locked, but he knows we're here. I guess the store is closed, but maybe he'll come talk to us.

NUCK: (pointing at the door) Maybe you try "pull" door, like sign say.

Smart alec.

I felt like an idiot but pulled on the door. It opened and smacked a little bell mounted to the top of the door frame. The bell rang, announcing that customers were entering the store. The old guy got up and greeted us. He was wearing a black top hat with feathers stuck under the hat band, a decorative native Indian pullover shirt, suede pants with fringe on the outer part of the legs and moccasins on his feet.

ME: Hi, we're looking for Mr. Squatting Platypus, the owner. Is that you?

SQUATTING PLATYPUS (SP): That depends. Do I owe you money?

ME: Uh, no.

SP: (smiling) Then yes, I'm Squatting Platypus. A strange name, I know. People jus' call me "Squat" or "Plat", so ya'll can do the same, either name. The store's closin' up, going out of business, but I still got some good pipe tobacco, cigars and homemade cigarettes if'n yer intrested.

ME: (shaking my head) No thanks, neither of us smoke. We're looking for two large metal figures that may have been at the front of your store. They were painted as native Indians. A guy named Bumpy said you had them and were interested in selling them because you were closing your store.

SP: Oh yes, Bumpy mentioned you'd come by. Well sir, if you wants to deal on my two big injuns a few things needs to happen. I needs to know theys goin' to a good home, we haf to agree on a price, and yer gonna haf to smoke a pipe with me and have a glass of swamp honey. It's tradition, a local drink.

NUCK: Drink have sting!

SP: (laughing) Why, yes it do! Ya'll had swamp honey? You know it's made from swamp water and wasp honey.

ME: No, never. We heard of it. A guy named Specky mentioned it. But we probably shouldn't drink alcohol or smoke anything. But look, wasps don't make honey. Bees make honey.

SP: This t'aint no bee honey. They's real wasps, swamp wasps. They make honey out in the swamp. But ya'll gotta have a sip and a smoke or we cain't seal a deal. If we cain't seal a deal, we got no deal. It's Cajun bayou tradition. Cain't break tradition.

I huffed and rolled my eyes. I'm not much of a drinker. I never have been. I'll occasionally have a beer or a mixed drink, but I usually never finish the drink. I was worried. I didn't want anything to do with a drink made from swamp water and wasp honey. I still didn't understand the wasp making honey thing.

As for smoking, I did that once in 1975, when I was 16 and trying to impress a girl. I smoked three cigarettes, and it caused me to throw up, violently – in front of the girl. When I throw up it's very loud. I can't help it. The girl wasn't impressed. I never tried smoking again. I never saw the girl again either. And here I was, all these years later, none too pleased that local tradition and protocol demanded that I had to smoke tobacco and drink swamp honey.

But I just HAD to get those two Nutcracker Soldiers. I'd traveled a long way and put in a lot of time. More importantly, the Soldiers were from Idora Park, and they HAD to come home with me even if I HAD to suffer a "sip and a smoke" to close the deal with Squatting Platypus.

Sure enough, "Squat" produced a peace pipe looking thing and a bottle of a yellow-tan syrupy looking liquid that I presumed to be swamp honey. The pipe resembled something from an old cowboy and Indian movie. It even had a couple of feathers attached. I was not looking forward to any of this. Squat set the items down on a table near us and offered us a seat.

NUCKED!

SP: Let's talk price on my two Indians, then we have a toke and a drink to celebrate.

ME: First, can I see the two Soldiers… er, I mean Indians? I just want to make sure they are what I'm hoping they are.

Squat nodded and beckoned that we follow. Nuck and I did as he said and after a couple of turns down a short hallway, we saw the two Nutcracker/Indians propped against a wall. There was no doubt in my mind, these were from Idora Park, and I HAD to have them. I nodded to Squat, and we walked back to the room we'd left earlier. Time to talk about the price, smoke a pipe and drink the wasp swill, unfortunately.

We talked price, we made a deal. I was fine with the compromise as was Squat. He lit the pipe, took a few puffs, then handed me the pipe. I was hesitant, but took two puffs, trying not to inhale, and handed the pipe to Nuck. The smoke had a hickory flavor to it. I coughed a few times but managed to survive. Nuck seemed okay too after he took a short drag. The swamp honey drink was next.

Squat reached into his vest and pulled out a notepad and pen, set them on the table and pushed them toward me.

ME: What's this? What are they for?

SP: Wasp honey kin numb the tongue a tad on some folk. The notepad is jus' a precaution.

ME: (confused) Wait a minute, is it really necessary to drink this stuff? I mean, we already agreed on the sale, and we smoked the pipe. Do we really have to drink that swamp stuff? Two out of three ain't bad!

SP: Sorry friend, cain't break an ancient ritual. Customs and courtesies must be honored. When in Rome you do as the Romans! But, why don't you go ahead and pay me now, then we'll have our little toast.

That should have worried me, but I wasn't thinking right. With the benefit of hindsight, I should have had the drink first, then paid him. Better yet, I should have faked it, put the drink to my lips and not drank. Instead, I paid him the agreed sum and then drank the swamp honey, but just a tiny sip. It wasn't that bad tasting, really.

The sting didn't hit me right away. It crept up on me then BANG! I could taste the honey part first and something sour that I guessed was probably the swamp water. I was thinking about the swamp water, hoping that they'd distilled it and that this stuff wouldn't make me go blind. I wondered if Cap'n Jack might have peed in the swamp, or do alligators do their toilet business on land?

That's what I was thinking about when the wasp sting walloped me good. It felt like something was buzzing in my mouth, like the wasps were in there flying around, just checking things out. Then they dived right in and hit me! It wasn't so much as a sting; it was like a hundred stings at once. I put my hands over my mouth. I could feel my tongue burning and swelling and my face was glowing red. I was sweating like crazy. Mostly, my mouth was on fire. I needed water, milk, something to stop this burning sting.

ME: (choking) wmuilb!

I didn't recognize the words coming from my own mouth. The stinging spread to my lips. They felt huge and rubbery, and they burned from the sting. My tongue felt like a giant chunk of soft burning rubbery stuff.

NUCK: What, boss?

ME: (choking, grabbing my throat) WMUILB! WMUILB!

Why was the room spinning? I put both hands on the table. Was I moving in slow motion or did the table get shorter? It took a long time for my hands to land on it. The room kept spinning, not in concentric circles, but in big, long oval loops, like a planet orbiting far from the sun, like Pluto. Thinking of Pluto's long looping circles made the room spin faster. I pushed Pluto from my mind and held onto the table.

NUCKED!

NUCK: (frowning) What you say?

ME: (panicked, desperate, trying to focus on Nuck's face) WMUILB MOW!!!

My eyes were watering like crazy. I thought about wiping them with my hand but opted not to. I'd touched that glass of hellfire with my hands. If I got that stuff in my eyes I might never see again. I could go blind. The thought of being blind caused me to imagine the horror of being on that lady's shooting range. I felt the gag reflex in my throat, and I fought it, tried to clear my mind so as not to throw up. The sting seemed to be spreading everywhere in my body now. How? I took one tiny sip! Why can't I communicate with these guys? I NEED water, now!

An idea hit me!

I could barely see, but I remembered a sink somewhere in the room. Point to the sink! There must be water there. They should understand that. But, where's the sink now? My eyes were so watery. I could barely see. A shot in the dark, just try pointing at something, anything. I attempted to raise my right arm to point where I guessed the sink might be. My arm didn't obey. It wanted to stay on the safety of the table. I commanded it to rise and stubbornly it did so, maybe a foot, maybe less. I couldn't tell.

ME: (pointing to God only knows where) WMUILB MOW! MOW! BRHY!

It took all I had to fight the spinning, looping room, my burning, rubbery mouth and lips and my watering eyes. But I think I did it. I think I had pointed out the sink. They should get the message now. I breathed a cautious sigh of relief and waited for one of them to bring me the cooling drink that might hopefully ease this terrible suffering. I laid my head on the table and waited. I could hear Nuck speak, but I couldn't see him through my watery eyes.

NUCK: Boss, what that mean?

WHAT THAT MEAN? What does he mean, "what that mean?" I was furious now! Why can't they understand? I'm burning from the inside out and I need water now!

ME: (desperate, shouting) WMUILB! BLRMB WMUILB! MOW! BRHY!

I was pleading, begging. The sounds coming from my mouth weren't the words I had formed in my brain, "WATER! BRING WATER! NOW! HURRY!" But no one was moving, and water wasn't coming.

SP: (smiling, self-satisfaction in his tone) Use the notepad, friend.

The notepad! Of course! I couldn't see it through my watering eyes, so I slid my right hand across the table to where Squat guy had set it. My hand moved in slow motion, but my fingers found the notepad and the pen. I summoned my left arm to assist the right hand and it begrudgingly did so. I scrawled something on the notepad that I hoped resembled "WATER NOW!" Success? I hoped so!

That's the last thing I remember before surrendering to the spinning room, feeling completely limp and blacking out...

Two days later we were well on our way home to Ohio with the two Indians/Nutcrackers tied down securely in the bed of my truck. I'd survived. I didn't remember drinking any water, but Nuck said he was able to decipher my "hierogoofic" writing and he retrieved a glass of water for me.

The Indians/Nutcrackers are on display now in our little museum, but no longer Indians. They are Nutcrackers again. I painted one of them to match the colors they wore when Idora Park closed in 1984. His blouse is dark blue. I painted the other Nutcracker with a red blouse like they were in the late 1950s and into the 1960s. One for each era. They look good.

It took a day and a half, but my tongue healed well, and I was able to speak normally again. Nuck took the swamp honey concoction like a champ. It didn't seem to affect him at all. When I was able to speak,

I asked him about that. He told me that being a ninja he religiously ingests a tiny amount of scorpion venom to build his resistance to poisons. I guess it's a ninja thing? He said the swamp honey tasted like Fargo Red soda pop without the fizz.

We never did see Bumpy again or Cap'n Jack the alligator. Squatting Platypus eventually closed shop completely. He mentioned moving farther south, maybe Miami. Who knows? We got what we were after.

SPIKE'S SIDE OF THE STORY

Sometimes I think Jim writes these stories just so he can channel his inner Charles Dickens and use the ridiculous names he creates. Swamp Honey certainly has a few: Bumpy, Squatting Platypus, Specky, Cross Eyed Willy and of course, Cap'n One Eyed Jack. I have no idea where he gets the inspiration. Although he might have stolen Cap'n One Eyed Jack from our one-eyed cat appropriately named, One Eyed Jack.

And the street names? Well, they were inspired by some of the finest misspelled road signs we've seen in our travels (mostly within five miles of our home).

We've done a lot of travel through the swamp lands of our country and both of us cringe as we do. As beautiful as the countryside is, it's also scary as all get out. Jim swrote this story when we were on a road trip that started in the Florida Everglades and took us to Louisiana. There's a lot of scary critters and just a few more than its fair share of crazy characters along those roads.

NUCKED!

Jim isn't much of a drinker. I on the other hand have been known to enjoy a cocktail… or two… or three. I'll often offer him a taste and most of the time he'll decline. But when he does try it, he usually makes a face that looks something like what I imagine tasting Swamp Honey would cause. He just doesn't like it. Except very expensive tequila… He likes very expensive tequila. And please don't offer him rum. We'll be picking him up off the floor (and rushing to a hospital) if he drinks rum. He has horrible reactions to rum which I'm sure had a role in his description of drinking Swamp Honey.

As for those Soldiers, they didn't come from Louisiana, but they might as well have been living in a swamp. Jim found them when he was pursuing a deal for another Idora Park artifact. As he walked around an out-building on his way to see the other artifact, he noticed the two Soldiers rotted and rusty, paint peeling off from years sitting unprotected out in the weather and sunken into the ground with mud up to their "ankles". A deal was made, the Soldiers came home.

Photos from Idora Park's Kiddieland show the Soldiers with two different paint patterns through the years. In some photos they have a blue outfit and in others a red. When we got them, they were red. Jim restored one to the blue uniform and left one red so that we could have a representation of both styles.

LIFE LESSON: Some deals are worth the pain

I think people believe creating The Idora Park Experience has been sexy and exciting. And in some ways, it has been. But it has also been painful and frustrating at times.

We've had to make deals with people who have disrespected us, lied to us, cheated us, tried to scam us, price gouged us and asked for terms from us that most people would have punched them for.

But we've always had to try to keep our wits about us and remember that what we do isn't about us. It's about the community and the people who loved Idora Park… and those who never knew Idora Park but deserve to know.

Before we opened the doors to The Idora Park Experience we realized what we had was something pretty special and we needed to find a way to share it. So, we built a building and opened the doors so that anyone who wanted to come see it could. It's been an amazing experience. One that reminds us that all those difficult and sometimes painful deals we had to make were worth it. And judging from the size of the crowds and comments we get when we open the museum, we believe the community appreciates it.

But all these years in, we still come across those who want to know "what we'll give them for (whatever Idora thingy they have)" and those who ask what the lowest is we'll take for some piece of merchandise they want from our store, and of course those who tell us what we "should" do, as if what we've done isn't enough.

As we write this, we are facing a new challenge. What will happen with this collection when we no longer curate it.

Neither of us ever imagined how difficult trying to give something away can be. But we'll keep trying… until we don't.

TERROR OVER MICHIGAN

I drove to Cleveland airport with Nuck. We were scheduled to catch a flight to Pepsatini, Minnesota. I'd never heard of Pepsatini until Nuck told me that Idora Park "gold" was located there.

Cleveland airport was a two-hour drive from our home in Canfield, Ohio. I was already tired after a very long day that included refurbishing an Idora Park Tilt-A-Whirl car, so I wasn't looking forward to driving for another two hours to get to Cleveland. I hoped that maybe I'd catch a nap on the plane if I could get Nuck to leave me alone for a while.

Our plane trip?

We were on a mission to get a 1931 Claw machine that had been at Idora's Penny Arcade.

Nuck's always on the lookout for Idora Park artifacts. He found the claw machine on a television show. No kidding! A fishing show!

NUCKED!

Nuck told me he was switching channels after watching a baking show. If you recall, Nuck is a member of the Amalgamated Union of Bakers and Ninjas, Local 867. As such, he is required to stay current with certain baking classes as well as ninja tactics. Strange, but that's his union. Who am I to question or judge?

Nuck said he had just put away his flour and measuring cups and was switching TV channels when, from the corner of his eye he caught the fishing show. An interviewer was asking questions of some local fisherman at a sportsmen's shop and as the camera scanned the shop, there in the background sat the Idora Park Claw machine. It was just a panning shot, but Nuck has the eyes of a hawk and recognized the machine immediately from an old photo we have.

Pam Dyce Cousins with the Idora Park Claw Machine

Once I was told about the "find" we located the story online, replayed the interview and re-examined the old Arcade photo. They were a match! The internet search also revealed the name of the fishing supply store. It was called "The Fishing Plaice", located in Pepsatini, Minnesota.

A phone call was made, a deal was struck with the owner, and we planned our mission to retrieve another long-lost artifact from Idora Park. The owner of the store told me over the phone that he'd bought the fishing store from the previous owner's wife when that man had passed away. The man had been from "somewhere" in Ohio. The Claw machine stayed in the store after the purchase as did everything else inside the store. The previous owner's family weren't interested in keeping anything in the store. The new owner, Oscar "Guppy" Chum had no connection to the Claw machine and said he'd be happy to sell it. He could use the space for more fishing supplies. We cut a deal.

That's why we are sitting at Gate #J5309 in Cleveland airport. The plan was to fly to Minnesota, buy the Claw machine, then rent a van and drive back to Ohio. The Claw machine was too large and cumbersome to bring it back on a plane. Renting a car was the only option.

Nuck and I sat together in the terminal. He wanted to chat as usual, but I was beat. I couldn't wait to get on the plane and take a short nap. I closed my eyes, half listening to whatever Nuck was going on about, cupcakes or Angel food icing methods or something he'd learned in his latest baking class. I wanted to rest, just for a few minutes.

I shifted my mind into cruise control, leaned my head back against my chair and eyes closed…

No such luck.

Our flight was called, and we headed to the departure area where we had to show our passports which was strange since this isn't an international flight. I had inquired about it over the phone when I paid for the tickets and received some weird answer about it being a requirement should the plane need to divert to Michigan. That didn't make sense to me either, but I've grown tired of life's constant silly battles and opted long ago to be more choosey on which ones to fight. I showed the boarding agent my passport.

Once our tickets were checked we went down a flight of stairs and found ourselves standing outside near an old military-looking plane. I've flown in and out of many places in more than a few locations around the planet and have on occasion had to walk outside a terminal to get to my plane. I thought it odd that it was happening in Cleveland, but even stranger was that the plane in front of me looked like a U.S. Air Force C130 cargo plane. It had four big turbo propeller-driven engines and the whole plane was painted olive drab green, a military color.

We had a full flight of 23 passengers, but I seemed to be the only person puzzled by the look of the plane. Everyone else just started walking right to the plane like it was the natural thing to do. Maybe they were used to this?

A baggage handler was slinging suitcases inside the rear ramp. I asked him if this was the flight to Pepsatini and he nodded a yes. I shrugged and climbed aboard the plane. Nuck followed me in. The seats were positioned sideways along the inside of the plane. They were exactly like the aircraft web seats I'd ridden in many times when I was in the military.

ME: (looking at Nuck) This is crazy! It's just like a military flight. I think this IS a military plane, or it used to be not too long ago. I guess this is what you get when you pay for a cheap flight. Sheesh!

It didn't take long before the plane was all buttoned up and ready to taxi. I was very apprehensive. This whole situation just felt so strange. There was no door to the flight deck where the pilots sat. I thought all planes had to have locked doors after 9/11. This plane didn't qualify? We could hear the pilots talking over the radio to the airport tower, getting taxi and runway clearance.

The plane soon rolled down the runway and took off, airborne without incident. The sound of those four engines was kind of loud inside the plane. I asked the flight attendant for earplugs, and she said she couldn't issue them "yet" because we were likely to fly over Michigan. Michigan? I wondered why we can't have earplugs over Michigan but was too dumbstruck to ask her and she was quickly off assisting another passenger with a pillow and blanket.

NUCK: Plane loud, boss! Maybe we get earplug?

ME: I just asked her for them, and she said she can't issue them because we're going to fly over Michigan. Weird.

NUCK: (puzzled) Why that so, boss?

ME: How should I know? Maybe it's an altitude or air pressure thing with the ears? I've got no idea. Everything about this flight is weird.

We looked at each other, both shrugged our shoulders and settled our heads back against the uncomfortable webbed upright of our seats. Thirty minutes later I heard and felt a "whump" outside the plane. The plane immediately jerked and reacted like a big gust of wind had knocked it sideways and upwards a few feet.

ME: (alarmed) I don't remember ever HEARING a wind gust outside a plane. I've felt them before, but that was loud.

Suddenly, there was another "whump" outside, and we rocked upwards a bit, then another "whump" that came from just behind, then another one that sounded like it was right behind me. Bird strikes? There was a port window behind Nuck. I climbed up out of my seat and looked outside. Another "whump"! I saw it near the plane's tail. The "whump" was a small black cloud that quickly disappeared. The look and sound reminded me of those old World War II movies where the allied planes on a bombing run were being fired at with ack ack or flak.

FLAK?!

Someone is shooting at us?!

I spun around, horrified, looking for the flight attendant. She was casually walking toward the front bulkhead, and with no sense of urgency or distress she casually picked up the microphone to make an announcement.

FLIGHT ATTENDANT: (speaking over the public address) We have just entered Michigan airspace. As a precaution we ask that each of you reach under your seat and place the protective flak jacket on your seat, then sit on it to protect your buttocks.

Flak jackets under our seats?

NUCKED!

Another "whump", then another. The "whumps" were coming more often now and the plane was being rocked from side to side, top to bottom and front to back. What is going on? Why aren't the pilots getting us out of here?

ME: (flabbergasted and looking at Nuck) Did she just say "flak jacket"?

NUCK: (laughing) She say "buttocks" too, boss!

ME: (angry, scared, confused) You think this is funny? What's funny? Someone's shooting at this plane, and no one here seems concerned!

NUCK: Boss, you concerned. Everyone else okay.

ME: (enraged) WE'RE NOT OKAY! SOMEONE IS SHOOTING AT US! WHAT IS THIS, AN EPISODE OF THE TWILIGHT ZONE?

I watched the other passengers calmly unclip their seatbelts, reach under their seats, place a flak vest in the seat, then sit back down and buckle their belt. No one seemed panicked or alarmed. They went back to reading newspapers, magazines, phones and tablets. What the heck is going on? We're being shot at and no one cares? Is this normal? How can this be normal? Nuck and I grabbed our flak vests and sat on them.

Suddenly, I heard the cockpit radio blare. It was obviously someone on the ground calling our plane.

VOICE: (calm, professional) Calling Ohio aircraft, Ohio aircraft, be advised, this is Michigan Ground Control. You have unlawfully entered Michigan airspace. We have initiated firing of our antiaircraft batteries.

We could hear our pilot respond on his radio.

PILOT: (calmly, in a matter-of-fact voice) Roger that, Michigan Ground Control. We have begun our climb to evade flak damage.

What the heck was that all about? It was so nonchalant. Michigan says "Hey, we're going to shoot you down." And our pilot says, "Oh, okay. We're going to try to get away. Talk to you later."???

The flight attendant saw and heard the commotion I was making, and she walked to where I was sitting. She maneuvered well across the plane despite the rocking from the incessant flak explosions.

FLIGHT ATTENDANT: (calm voice) Sir, you're going to alarm the other passengers. Please stay seated, remain calm and lower your voice.

ME: CALM? HOW ARE ANY OF YOU CALM? WE'RE BEING SHOT OUT OF THE SKY! NO ONE SHOULD BE CALM!

Flight Attendant: Oh, don't be silly! This is Michigan. No way they can hit us. They still use ack ack ammo from pre-World War II! We evade them all the time. In fact, …

She didn't get to finish.

"WHUMP!" Then immediately, "BANG!" and the sound of metal being torn violently from the plane. I could hear it shredding away, screeching and slamming against the side of the plane, then suddenly it must have broken completely away, scratching its way down the length of the plane. I hoped it would fall and hit that Michigan control tower. Suddenly, we're in a new ballgame and everyone on the plane finally took an interest.

A calm, automated voice alarm started blaring from the cockpit, "WARNING! HULL BREACH! WARNING! HULL BREACH!"

You think???

ME: (panicked) HULL BREACH?! This is crazy! Why are they shooting at us?

Meanwhile, the "whumps" just kept on coming, hot and heavy every second or so.

The flight attendant ran, yes ran over to the side of the plane where all the noise came from, looked out a port hole, then ran to the microphone.

FLIGHT ATTENDANT: (sounding almost relieved) Everything is under control folks, we just lost one of our outboard engines, but there's no need to be alarmed. We still have three good engines, and this plane is capable of flying with only one engine. Unfortunately, the engine loss will delay our arrival to Pepsatini by an hour.

There were some passenger groans because of the extra hour delay. But the flight attendant's calm demeanor seemed to assure nearly everyone that all was otherwise okay, and they all went back to their newspapers, magazines, phones and tablets. But not everyone was pacified.

ME: We LOST an engine? Don't you mean we had an engine SHOT OFF?

FLIGHT ATTENDANT: (hushing me) We still have three good engines and we're climbing out of danger.

ME: Why are we in danger in the first place? Michigan is part of the United States of America, key words "UNITED" and "STATES"! We're supposed to be allies! No, we're more than allies. Well, except for football season, but that's just football, not war! Ohio is not at war with Michigan, so why are they shooting at us?

Before she could answer the next "whump" followed with another loud "BANG", then immediately another "whump-bang" and I thought the whole plane was going to flip over.

ME: (frantic, yelling) Now what? They've got us zeroed in, don't they? That's it for us, we're toast!

The flight attendant ran to my side of the plane to look out the port hole, then the opposite side of the plane to do the same. The passengers looked up, seemingly more concerned, but not panicked.

What's up with these people? Are they drugged? Who reacts like this when they're about to die?

FLIGHT ATTENDANT: (on the intercom again) Passengers, I regret to inform you that we have lost two more of our engines. We still have one perfectly functioning engine, but the loss of the other two engines is going to delay our arrival to Pepsatini by an additional two hours. Our arrival time is expected to be…

NUCK: (interrupting her) Three-hour delay, three engine? We lose numba four engine we up here all day!

ME: Uh, no. It doesn't work like that. We lose number four engine we reach the ground immediately!

Then, the unthinkable happened, "whump-bang" and the screech of metal. For just a few seconds there was total silence. No engine noises. The plane slowly began to nose downward. I saw the pilot and co-pilot walk back toward the rear door. They were wearing parachutes. The Flight Attendant was donning one too. She was scrambling to catch up with the pilots. The door opened and out they went, one at a time.

NUCK: Where they go, boss? Who fly plane?

I felt the nose of the plane dipping farther downward and we started accelerating and spinning toward the ground. We were all pinned to the sides of the plane. The plane made a high-pitched howling sound just like a German World War II Stuka plane in a dive bomb run.

I started screaming, "THIS IS IT! WE'RE ALL GONNA DIE! THE PLANE IS GOING DOWN! WE'RE ALL DEAD! GOD HELP US!"

I felt myself being shaken, hard. I turned to look at Nuck. I tried to focus.

NUCK: Boss, boss, wake up! You scare everyone in airport! People cancel flight 'cause of you!

ME: (confused) What? Where's the plane? We're not crashing?

NUCK: Boss, you dream! We still in airport!

ME: We're not in the plane?

NUCK: No, I tell you already! We in airport. People mad at you!

I looked around the room. He was right. I must have nodded off in the departure area. We were still in the airport. There was no plane, no crash. It was all a bad dream after all. I had fallen asleep! No plane crash!

ME: (wiping drool from my chin, rubbing my eyes) There's hardly anyone at this gate anymore. People are mad at me? Why? Was I snoring? Did we miss the flight?

NUCK: No, boss! Flight cancel! Everyone hear you scream, "WE ALL DIE! WAAAA!" People scared, cancel flight, airline cancel flight too. You in big trouble. Security coming for you, on way here now!

ME: (panicked, reality sinking in) Uh, oh! We've gotta get out of here! Run! We'll get my truck out of short-term parking and drive to Pepsatini instead.

And that's what we did. It took much longer to drive than it would have taken to fly, but we didn't have to pass through Michigan at all! No flak!

We stopped at a hotel near Chicago for the night, then made it to Pepsatini the next day and picked up the old Idora Park Claw machine. One more hotel stay on the return trip, and we made it home safely.

I think it best if I avoid Cleveland Airport for a while, just in case.

What of the Claw Machine? It's a 1931 Electro-Hoist made by Star Machine Manufacturing of New York City and it's safe and sound in our little museum. Seriously, it is. I wouldn't give you any flak about that.

SPIKE'S SIDE OF THE STORY

We've established that Jim likes to collect Idora stuff (you wouldn't be reading this book if he didn't), and I like to travel. Our bargain is, I put up with the Idora stuff and he puts up with my travel bug tendencies. Luckily, many times, those two passions meet in the middle, and we travel far and wide for Idora stuff.

Almost always that means a trip in the RV or if it's less than a day's drive round-trip a quick jaunt in our pickup. This story was written on one of those very long RV trips. Probably so long that he wished we'd just flown.

But collecting Idora artifacts rarely, if ever, includes air travel. After reading this story, I think I'm glad it doesn't. We have however, done quite a bit of air travel. Which, mixed with Jim's very loud and obnoxious snoring can be a real treat for anyone sitting near him. It is however, quite entertaining when he suddenly wakes himself up from his own loud snoring. He'll quickly look around to see if anyone else noticed. Which of course they didn't because they are sleeping and snoring too.

When Jim was in the Air Force, he traveled extensively for missions he wasn't allowed to talk about. That is until the movie "Charlie Wilson's War" told the story for all to know. I must admit it was pretty interesting watching the movie and suddenly realizing that it was about what he had been doing on those missions. You'll have to watch the movie to get the story, but it included escorting plane loads of weapons that the government said we didn't have, and delivering them to countries and militias the government said we weren't supporting...

There was also the time when he was sitting on the flight deck with the flight crew during a mission and the plane was cruising at about 300 feet altitude, when suddenly the control tower advised the pilot to take evasive maneuvers because there was a 1,000-foot mountain directly in front of them. The plane warning systems began blaring the instructions to "PULL UP! HONK-HONK! PULL UP! HONK-HONK!". Jim and the rest of the crew knew they were gonners, but the pilot managed to climb quickly enough that they cleared the mountain. (Obviously, or we wouldn't be spending this little bit of time together.)

I'm sure all of these life-highlighting experiences, and a few others he's had, contributed to this little terror over Michigan adventure (as did his passion for Ohio State Football and disdain for anything Michigan). Oh, and maybe we've watched a few too many TV shows about air disasters...

But most of all, I think his sense of humor is just a little whacked and left with idle hands and mind, he'll take a quick nap, and when he wakes, this is the kind of story he'll create.

As for the real story as to how we got that 1931 Claw Machine... we bought it from someone right here in Canfield.

LIFE LESSON: Imagination is different for everyone

It's one of the hardest things in the world for me to do. Be imaginative. For Jim, it comes naturally, as we can all see... or read.

When someone says draw a picture, I draw the same darn picture I've been drawing since my very first memory of being asked to draw, about 55 years ago. A simple house, one flower in the yard that has just a few petals and a couple of leaves, a shining sun and a stick figure.

Hmmmm... now that I look at it, that stick figure might be gender neutral... Geez, I was way ahead of my time. I'm sure a psychologist would have a field day with this drawing, or the fact that it hasn't changed much in 55 years. But I don't think I have to worry too much about it... in the context of our lives... a little bit of simplicity is very welcome.

On the other hand, ask Jim to draw a picture and you'll end up with a set of mechanical drawings of some invention that's still

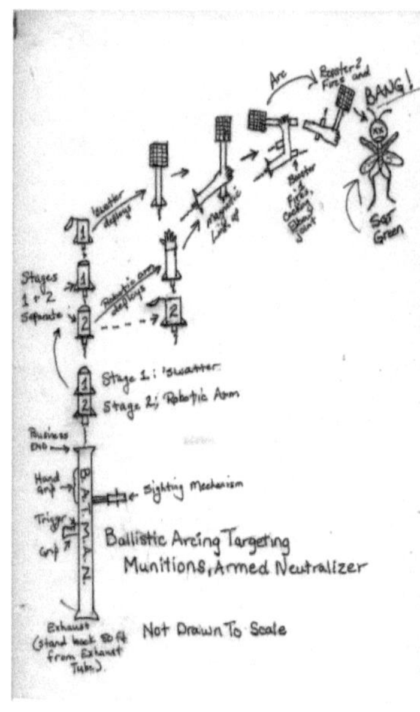

waiting to happen – I offer the B.A.T.M.A.N. as evidence (a "NUCKED!" reference).

… Ask me to tell a story and you'll get "Once upon a time they lived happily ever after." We all know what we get when Jim is asked to tell a story… Lunacy!

But I've learned through the years that imagination is different for everyone. And, while I may not be able to draw a detailed (or spatially accurate) picture, or weave a tale of adventure and laughs, my style of imagination is just as important.

I am the one who imagined retiring early and doing The Idora Park Experience Museum (although it didn't take much to convince Jim). I am the one who imagines great travel adventures and then plans the details about where to go, what to see, etc. And I am the one who spends night and day figuring out how to let Jim run rampant with his imagination and not get either of us in jail, sued or broke… Well, that might still be a work in progress.

So be imaginative… whatever that looks like for you.

THE TIME TUNNEL

Nope, not the 1966 – 67 TV show starring James Darren.

We'd heard a rumor that a tunnel was located under the now foliage-covered space below the Fun House. The Fun House burned to the ground in 1986 so no trace of the building remains. We needed to check out the tunnel rumor.

After tromping around out there for half an hour I turned to tell Nuck that this mission was a bust and maybe we should go home or go check out the old Helter Skelter site, that's what the bumper cars were named. But when I turned left, then right, then spun around in a 360 he was nowhere in sight. No Nuck. I figured that maybe he went somewhere to relieve himself. I walked in the direction that I'd last seen him and I promptly fell through an opening in the ground!

I landed on my feet, then my butt. I checked myself for injuries, but luckily, I was just a little scraped where my left arm rubbed something on the way down. It was dark down there, but when I looked up I could see daylight from the hole I'd fallen through. I hoped my eyes would adjust enough to the darkness so that I could see where I was and how I was going to get out.

I started to imagine bugs and snakes and things in there with me, maybe a rabid raccoon or angry squirrel. I decided that the smart thing to do was to yell for Nuck. He could get a rope and pull me out. I remembered my cell phone. I keep it in my back pocket. Luckily, it wasn't damaged. I could call Nuck on my phone if I could get a signal and I figured the phone's built-in flashlight would be a great help in exploring this space.

ME: (looking up through the hole, yelling) NUCK! NUCK! WHERE ARE YOU? I NEED YOUR HELP! I FELL IN A HOLE! GO GET A ROPE!

I turned when I heard movement behind me. A beam of light blinded me. I couldn't see who or what was behind the light.

NUCK: (annoyed, flashlight in hand) Why you yell, boss? I right here!

ME: You knucklehead, why didn't you warn me about the hole in the ground? I could have helped you get out. Now we're both stuck down here. I think I cut my arm too. I might need a tetanus shot now.

I pulled out my phone to check for a signal. No luck.

NUCK: (pointing) Not stuck. Look, ladder. It strong. I check.

ME: But you didn't think to tell me to watch out for the hole before I fell into it?

NUCK: Sorry, boss. Thought maybe you smart, watch where you walk.

ME: (ignoring the comment) So, I guess this is the secret tunnel? Or is it a basement? Have you looked around much?

NUCK: (smiling) No, I wait for you to drop in.

ME: Well, let's check it out.

NUCK: (pointing) Stack of old paper on work bench.

ME: (excited) Shine that light on the work bench! I need to see it! It's so dark in here. I can't believe I forgot a flashlight. I'm glad you thought to bring one.

NUCK: Flashlight required equipment. Union say so.

ME: Well, for once I'm in agreement with your union.

NUCK: (pointing) Old paper not newspaper, maybe blueprint.

ME: (surprised) Blueprints? No way!

Nuck shined the light toward the workbench, and we carefully picked our way in that direction, stepping over and around broken old boards and concrete strewn on the floor, likely debris from the Fun House fire and demolition.

I reached the bench and gently picked up a sheath of old papers. Nuck shined his light on them while I gingerly leafed through. They were blueprints all right! Blueprints to the Kooky Castle, dated 1972! I was shocked, these were original blueprints! How did they survive down here for nearly 40 years? How did no-one find them before us? Are we the first persons to find this place? And why were the blueprints left here when Idora Park closed in 1984? I searched through another stack of blueprints and found the plans for the Whacky Shack, dated 1968!

NUCK: (pointing) Boss, tunnel.

ME: You're right! These blueprints are such an amazing find. We'll come back for them, but let's check out that tunnel!

In the 1950s the Heidelberg Gardens (beer garden and lunchroom) building was raised above its foundation for a repair shop to be built under it. Kiddieland was built in 1951 in the upper Midway, on the site where the swimming pool once sat. Those kids' rides were going to need repair eventually, hence the new repair shop under the Heidelberg which was close to Kiddieland. It appears that management also added a tunnel under the Fun House! Another repair facility? But why? Where it led, we didn't know.

We started down the tunnel, Nuck leading the way with his flashlight. I was cursing myself for forgetting mine, but at least my phone provided some light. Suddenly, Nuck stopped dead in his tracks and motioned for me to stop. He played the flashlight across the ground in front of him.

NUCK: (warily) Bone, boss! Bone and skull.

ME: (surprised) What are they from? A squirrel, raccoon, groundhog?

NUCK: (frightened) No, boss! Look like baby with big teeth!

ME: (disbelieving) Baby? What? Give me that flashlight!

I grabbed the flashlight from his hand and swept it over the area where he pointed. There were three complete skeletons laying side by side! The hair on my neck and arms stood straight up. I bent to look closer at the bones, careful not to disturb them.

ME: Nuck, do you know what these are?

NUCK: (excited) I already tell you, boss! Bone and skull!

ME: Yes, but these are primate bones and skulls! Monkeys! These must be three of the monkeys that escaped from Idora's Monkey Island and were never caught. There were supposed to be four of them that got away. The great Monkey Escape of 1947! But how could they be missing since 1947 and remain hidden for the next 37 years while Idora remained open? Surely someone would have seen and reported wild monkeys at some point between 1947 and 1984. A monkey's lifespan is about 40 years. So, these three monkeys could be the original escapee monkeys or their offspring. But how did they stay hidden from park employees? Were they pets? The bones look like they've been laying here a long, long time so maybe they died soon after their escape? Maybe the bones have been here since 1947. What happened to the fourth monkey?

I didn't see or hear the movement behind us, but Nuck being a ninja seems to have a hundred eyes and uncanny hearing. He's also amazingly agile and quick. He heard something move behind us, and he started to turn which caused me to turn as well. Nuck is super fast. He has to be because he's a ninja. But he wasn't fast enough on this day. I'd seen him in action many times and no-one and no thing has ever gotten the drop on him. This day was different. The creature was big, and it was fast. Faster than anything I'd ever seen, so fast that it was a blur. It was upon Nuck's back, twisting him in an attempt to make him lose his balance and bring him to the ground. The flashlight on my phone caught the creature's fierce angry face in its light. Nuck went down helplessly, the huge creature on top of him, its arm raised high, the sharp claws from its hairy hand coming down fast…

A WARNING FROM SPIKE

You know how when you go to the zoo, and you see signs everywhere warning you not to feed the animals…?

Well, consider this your warning…

Our fans asked Jim to write a book of his stories… he wrote two…

See what happens when you feed the beast… you get more malarky.

As for Nuck, well only time will tell if our little buddy sees the light of day again…

ACKNOWLEDGEMENTS
All are honorary members of the
Amalgamated Union of Bakers and Ninjas,
Local#867

Once again, a massive thank you to our beautiful niece, Aaliyah Groves who made her modeling debut appearing as "Nuck" in the first "NUCKED!" book and continued her portrayal of our mischievous and very much-loved ninja in "NUCKED! 2". We thank her parents; our nephew Tim Groves, and his wife LeeAnn for generously sharing their love and support as well as their daughter's time and talent with us.

The Idora Park Experience wouldn't be what it is without the enduring support of our very dear friends and sounding boards for all our crazy ideas, Larry and Linda Cadman. They share our passion and mission to recover, restore and share all things Idora Park and have stepped up and helped us to prepare and present almost all our major events. We would have packed it up a long time ago had we not had their time, labor and love to see us through. We are thankful for them always being there for whatever the day may bring.

John Kost and Dana Eyer, where do we begin? They have no connection whatsoever to Idora Park or the Youngstown area. Yet, they travel from North Carolina (or wherever they happen to be) just to be a part of The Idora Park Experience and a part of our lives. For this, and their friendship, we feel incredibly blessed. We can't wait to see what life has in store for them…

Joe Sander, Joe Merritt and the students of MCCTC: We've partnered on seven projects with them; Chip the Turtle, Hootie the Hooterville Highway car, Jumbo the Lost River Elephant, the Kooky Castle car and Tower, the Kiddieland Mercedes car and the Cushman maintenance car, and each one has been a learning experience and a joy… We're thankful for them always giving us something to look forward to and for reminding us that a memory is simply a thought about the past until you find a way to bring it to the present and then share it with the future. That's when it becomes something legendary and, in some cases, a legacy.

Cory Nester and Paul Clapham: A Baker and Ninja of the highest level. They were the stars of the Elephant Escapade and are very dear friends, who once again, have no connection to Idora Park or the Youngstown area. But curiosity and lack of better judgement got ahold of them, and they jumped in with both feet to help us rescue Jumbo the Lost River Elephant and then showed up in July 2022 to help us prepare for, manage and recover from The Idora Park Experience opening that year. Oh, and they took on organizing a hoarders storage area into a craftsman's workshop. These two always seem to work miracles wherever they go and we're thankful they decided to bring that magic into our lives.

Terry and John Brennan: Jumbo might not have ever made it out of that field if it weren't for Baker Terry and Ninja John's time, labor and brains in the Elephant Escapade. We're grateful for their help and friendship. Not everyone changes their big travel plans to help rescue a decaying fiberglass elephant from an overgrown, muddy field.

We are grateful for who have given us clues, phone numbers, addresses, etc… so that we could find lost Idora Park artifacts, and to those who donated artifacts, shared stories, and helped us to share our story and the story of Idora Park, volunteered their time and labor, and most of all, visited The Idora Park Experience (and parted with their hard-earned cash to support our mission). Without them, The Idora Park Experience would not exist.

And finally, our sincere thanks to the unnamed individual who provided us with so much fodder for the two "NUCKED!" books and has always been happy to take our cash through the years, thanks for the memories… and laughs.

About Idora Park, the Ameys & The Idora Park Experience

Idora Park opened in 1899 as a picnic area located at the final trolley stop on the south side of Youngstown, Ohio. Over the years it expanded into a full-blown amusement park and home to the largest Ballroom between New York City and Chicago. It wasn't uncommon to have upwards of thirty thousand people turn out to see top name acts perform at the park.

On April 26, 1984, at the age of 85, it all went up in smoke… literally. A fire destroyed the two premier rides and half of one midway. Idora Park never recovered. It had one final season and then the gates closed and everything of value was auctioned off leaving only the broken bones of the park behind. Across the next thirty years mother nature, with a bit of help from scavengers and treasure hunters, reclaimed her own, eventually leaving no sign that Idora Park ever existed. Until Jim and Toni Amey came along…

Like so many Youngstown natives, Jim spent much of his

childhood at Idora Park, an amusement park located on the city's south side. In 1976 at the age of eighteen, with no local job prospects at hand, Jim joined the military and left Youngstown. It would be 17 years before he'd walk the grounds of Idora Park again and by that time, it had been dead almost 10 years.

Trespassing onto the old Idora Park property (It's okay, everyone does it), Jim and his wife Toni (he calls her Spike, but that's another story…) were shocked and heartbroken to see Youngstown's beloved Idora Park abandoned, dilapidated and disappearing from existence.

The Ameys spent the next 20 years collecting "stuff" from Idora Park as a way of holding on to the memories. What started out as an event poster, ticket stub, or game prize, here and there, eventually became parts to rides and structures and a full-blown obsession (aka passion). Along the way, they met some amazing (and oftentimes odd) people and had some crazy and unbelievable adventures.

Their experiences along with the realization that they had inadvertently become the curators of a large part of the heart, soul and joy that was once Youngstown, led them to believe there must be a higher purpose to what they were doing… otherwise, they were just hoarders. They knew they needed to find a way to share their experiences and collection with others.

In 2013 they built a 4,400 square foot building next to their home in Canfield, Ohio, to house the enormous collection of Idora Park artifacts and in April of 2014, 30 years after the fire that destroyed Idora Park, they welcomed over 1,000 people to the grand opening weekend of The Idora Park Experience.

Because of local zoning issues, the museum only opens a few days each year but has had more than 10,000 visitors to date and enjoys a large social media following.

The Ameys are the authors of the book, "Nucked! Misadventures with The Idora Park Experience Ninjas" published in 2021 and "Lost Idora Park," published in 2019 by Arcadia Publishing.

www.ingramcontent.com/pod-product-compliance
Lightning Source LLC
Chambersburg PA
CBHW031533150726
47990CB00001B/156